Learn to Code

Practice Book 2

Written by
Claire Lotriet

Published by

RISING STARS

Rising Stars UK Ltd, 7 Hatchers Mews, Bermondsey Street, London SE1 3GS
www.risingstars-uk.com

Published 2015

Author: Claire Lotriet
Computing consultant: Miles Berry
Text design: Words and Pictures Ltd, London
Typesetting: Words and Pictures Ltd, London
Cover design: Burville-Riley Partnership
Publisher: Becca Law
Editorial: Jenny Draine
Project manager: Estelle Lloyd
Illustrations: Eva Sassin, Advocate Art

Photo acknowledgements: pages 8–10, 12–14, 16–18, 20–22: screenshots from Scratch
http://scratch.mit.edu licensed under Creative Commons licence. Scratch is developed by
the Lifelong Kindergarten Group at the MIT Media Lab; pages 24–26, 28–30, 32–34, 36–38:
screenshots from Light Bot 2.0 www.light-bot.com; pages 40–42, 44–46, 48–50, 52–54:
screenshots from thimble.webmaker.org/ all used with permission; pages 49–50: map
data © Google 2015.

Rising Stars is grateful for the following people and their schools who contributed to the
development of these materials: Matt Rogers, Snowsfields Primary School; Dawn Hallybone,
Oakdale Junior School; Marc Faulder, Burton Joyce Primary School; Martyn Soulsby, North
Lakes School; John Janowski, Royal Russell Junior School.

British Library Cataloguing in Publication Data.
A CIP record for this book is available from the British Library.

ISBN: 978-1-78339-342-8

Printed by Newnorth Ltd, Bedford

Contents

How to use this book

Learning to code can seem like learning a new language! This book will show you how to code using three different tools. You will make your own games and web pages!

BOOK 2

The step-by-step instructions explain what you need to do.

8 On line 12, click between the *
* tag and *KS1*. Type in **<strong>**. Now click after the colon (after *KS1*). Type the closing tag **</strong>**.

```
Editor
1  <!doctype html>
2  <html>
3    <head>
4      <meta charset="utf-8">
5      <title>Sports Day information</title>
6    </head>
7    <body>
8      <h1> Sports day information</h1>
9      <p>Find out all you need to know</p>
10     <h2>Dates and Times</h2>
11     <p><strong>Date:</strong> Monday 1st July
12       <br><strong>KS1:</strong> 9:30-11:00am
13       <br>KS2: 1:30-3:00pm</p>
14   </body>
15 </html>
16
```

9 On line 13, click between the *
* tag and *KS2*. Type in **<strong>**. Now click after the colon (after *KS2*). Type the closing tag **</strong>**.

```
Editor              Undo    Redo
1  <!doctype html>
2  <html>
3    <head>
4      <meta charset="utf-8">
5      <title>Sports Day information</title>
6    </head>
7    <body>
8      <h1>Sports Day information</h1>
9      <p>Find out all you need to know</p>
10     <h2>Dates and Times</h2>
11     <p><strong>Date:</strong> Monday 1st July
12       <br><strong>KS1:</strong> 9:30-11:00am
13       <br><strong>KS2:</strong> 1:30-3:00pm</p
14   </body>
15 </html>
```

This text shows what you need to type in.

This text shows the words you'll see on the screen.

10 On line 9, click in front of the word *all*. Type **<em>**. Then click after the word *all* and type the closing tag **</em>**.

Any text between the *<em>* tags will be shown in italics.

```
Editor
1  <!doctype html>
2  <html>
3    <head>
4      <meta charset="utf-8">
5      <title>Sports Day information</title>
6    </head>
7    <body>
8      <h1> Sports day information</h1>
9      <p>Find out <em>all</em> you need to
   know</p>
10     <h2>Dates and Times</h2>
11     <p><strong>Date:</strong> Monday 1st July
12       <br><strong>KS1:</strong> 9:30-11:00am
13       <br><strong>KS2:</strong> 1:30-3:00pm</p
14   </body>
```

Handy tips give you extra help.

11 Finally, click before the final bracket in the *<h2>* tag and type so it reads **<h2 style="color:green;">**. Now select all the text on the page. Right-click and click on **Copy**. Then paste it into a document in Word or similar and save it to use next time.

```
Editor
1  <!doctype html>
2  <html>
3    <head>
4      <meta charset="utf-8">
5      <title>Sports Day information</title>
6    </head>
7    <body>
8      <h1>Sports Day Information</h1>
9      <p>Find out <em>all</em> you need to know</p>
10     <h2 style="color:green;">Dates and Times</h2>
11     <p><strong>Date:</strong> Monday 1st July
12       <br><strong>KS1:</strong> 9:30-11:00am
13       <br><strong>KS2:</strong> 1:30-3:00pm</p>
14   </body>
15 </html>
16
```

42

This text shows the commands you need to use in the program.

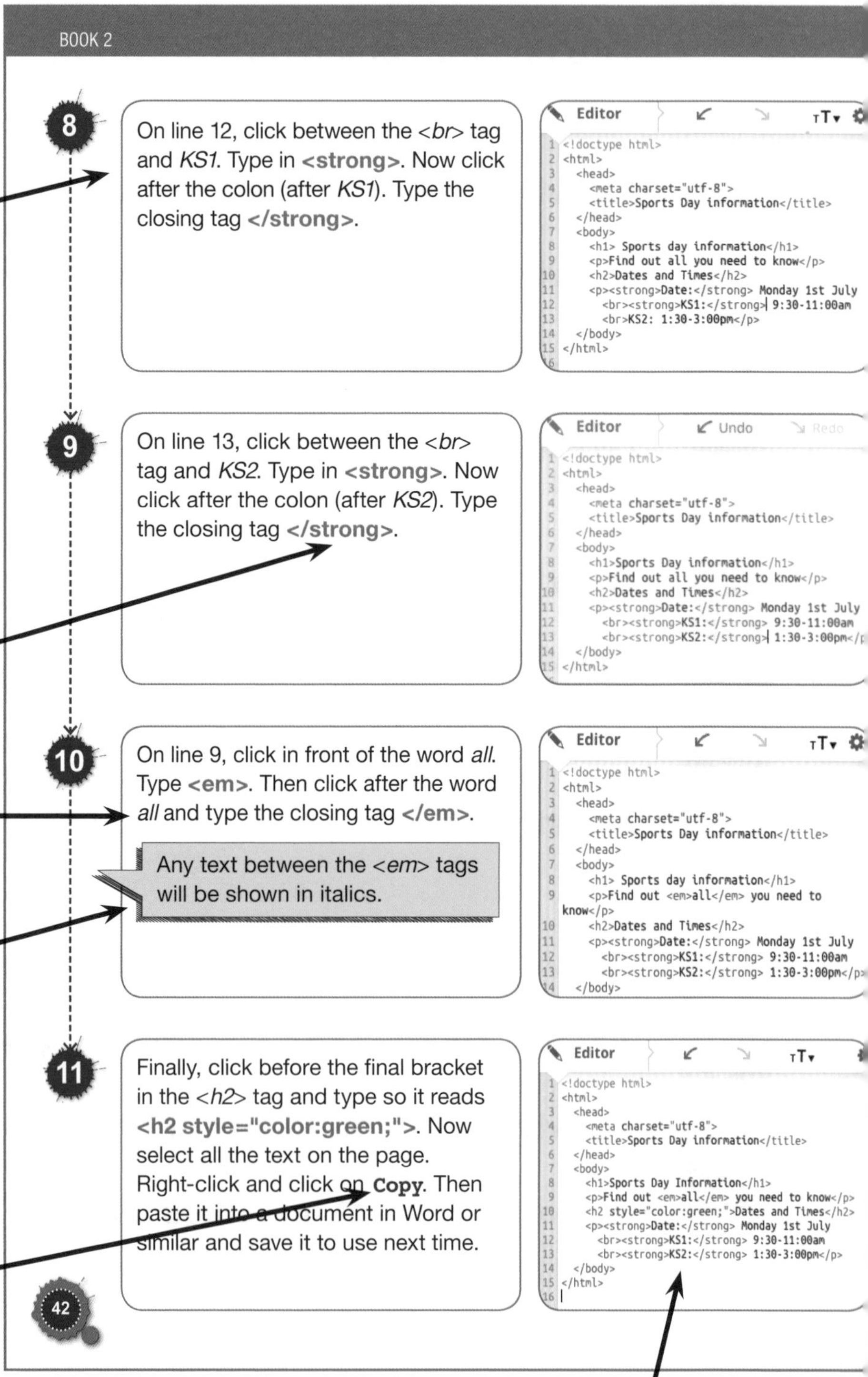

The pictures show what you should see on your screen.

This book uses three tools: Scratch, Lightbot and Thimble. Work your way through the activities for each tool in order. Each activity builds on the previous one.

Now try this . . .

- Can you make the *Dates and Times* heading smaller by swapping the *<h2>* tags for *<h3>* ones? The *<h3>* tag will display the text as a smaller heading.

- Can you display other words you want to stand out using the *<em>* tag?

- Can you change the colour of the *Dates and Times* subheading from green to another colour?

- Can you change the colour of the main heading?

- Design a web page of your own. What will it be about? Decide what headings, text and images you would like to include and where they would go on the page.

Take your learning further by trying these extra challenges!

These activities help you develop your understanding of coding away from the computer.

Key words

Can you explain to a partner what these words mean?

tag   **HTML**   **opening tag**   **closing tag**

These are important words that you need to understand. You can find definitions in the glossary on page 56.

How did you do?

Think about what you did in this activity. Did you:

- create a structured web page with different levels of text in it?
- change the code to make the *Dates and Times* heading smaller?
- use the *<em>* tag to display certain text in italics?
- change the code to change the colour of the *Dates and Times* heading?
- change the colour of the main heading?

Use these questions to review what you have learned in the activity.

43

Writing code to make something happen is exciting, but sometimes your code won't work as well as it could, or it won't work at all!

What happens when your code doesn't do what you want it to? You need to fix it!

The process of making our code better, or correcting mistakes (removing bugs in the code) is called debugging.

If you find a problem with your code, try to solve it yourself first, before asking a grown-up. The coding monsters are here to help you!

When you have finished writing your code, always run your program or script to see if it works.

Go through your code step by step in your head. Try to predict what will happen. Can you spot any mistakes?

for coding

Try explaining each bit of your code to a partner. Does it all make sense?

Try explaining your code to a rubber duck. Rubber duck debugging is used by proper programmers to fix errors in their code!

Show your code to a partner. Do they have any ideas about how to fix code that isn't working?

Activity 1: Scratch Programming using broadcast blocks

Sprites can use broadcast blocks to 'send' invisible messages to each other. In this activity you will use broadcast blocks to build buttons that draw different shapes when clicked.

1 Open Scratch: **www.scratch.mit.edu**. Click *Create* to start. Right-click on the cat sprite and click **delete**. Click on the **Paint new sprite** / icon. Now find the *New costume* section and click on the **choose costume from library** ☻ icon.

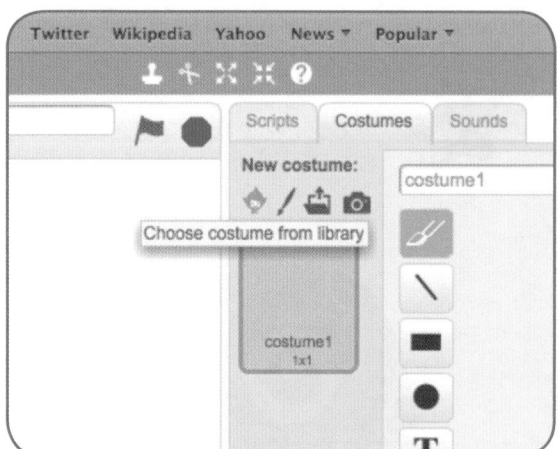

2 In the *Costume Library*, click on **Things** and then on **button3-a**. Click **OK**. In the bottom right corner of the scripts area, check it says *Vector Mode*; if not, click on **Convert to Vector**. Click on the **Text** Ⓣ tool. Type **Square** in the button and make the text red.

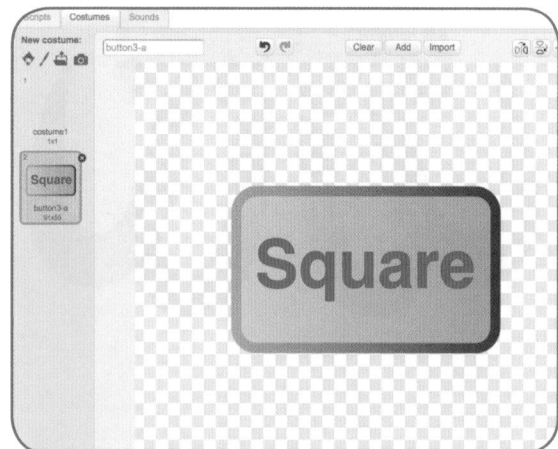

3 Right click on *Sprite 1* and choose duplicate. Click on *Sprite 2* and change the label to **Rectangle**. Move both button sprites to the top left of the preview window.

> Use the arrow button to drag the corner of the text box so the word *Rectangle* fits in the button.

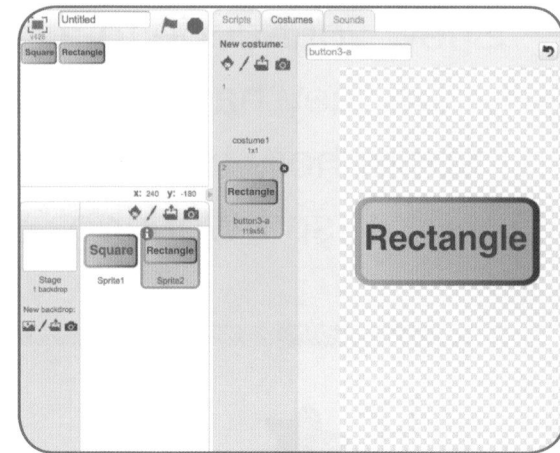

4 Click on the `Paint new sprite` ∕ icon. Now click on the `Choose costume from library` ✿ icon. Click on `Things` in the menu. Select `pencil-a` and click `OK`. Click on the `Set costume center` ⊞ button and drag the cross so it meets the pencil point.

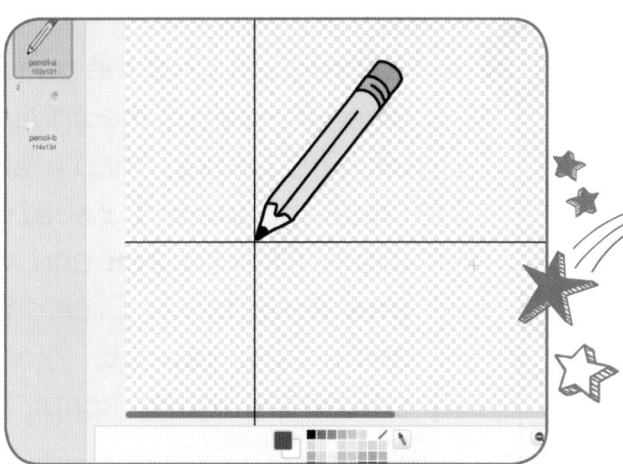

5 In the *Sprites* box, click the square button sprite. In the `Scripts` tab, click on `Events`. Drag a `when this sprite clicked` block into the scripts area. Snap a `broadcast message1` block under it. Click on the arrow and then `new message....` Type **Square** and click `OK`.

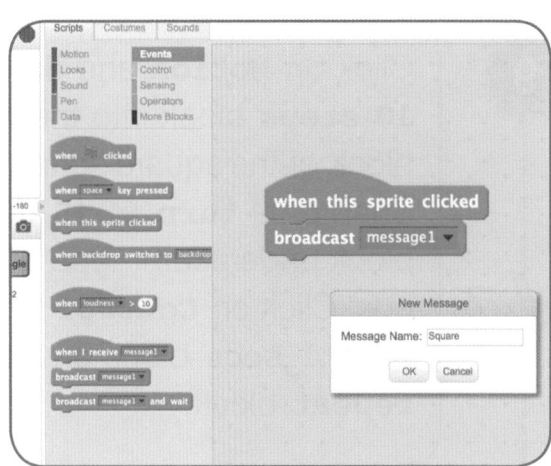

6 In the *Sprites* box, click the rectangle button sprite. In the `Scripts` tab, click on `Events`. Drag a `when this sprite clicked` block into the scripts area. Snap on a `broadcast...` block underneath. Click on the arrow and then `new message....` Type **Rectangle** and click `OK`.

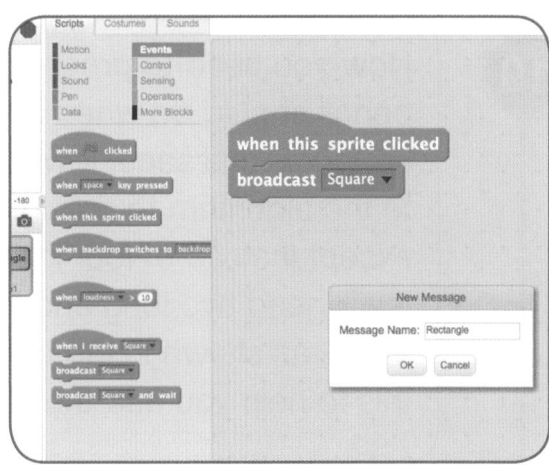

7 Click on the `pencil-a` sprite. Drag a `when` ⚑ `clicked` block into the scripts area. In the `Scripts` tab, click on `Looks`. Snap on a `hide` block. Click back on `Events` and drag across two `when I receive...` blocks. Click on the drop-down menu in one and select `Square`.

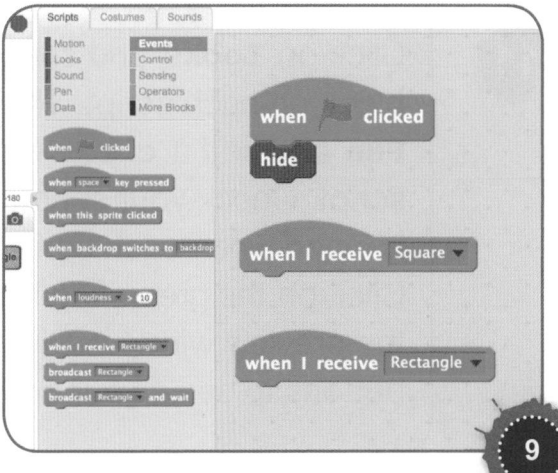

8

To program what the pencil does when it receives the *square* message, click on **Looks**. Snap a **show** block under the **when I receive Square** block. Click on **Pen** and snap on a **pen down** block. Click on **Control** and snap a **repeat...** block on. In the box on the square script, type **4**.

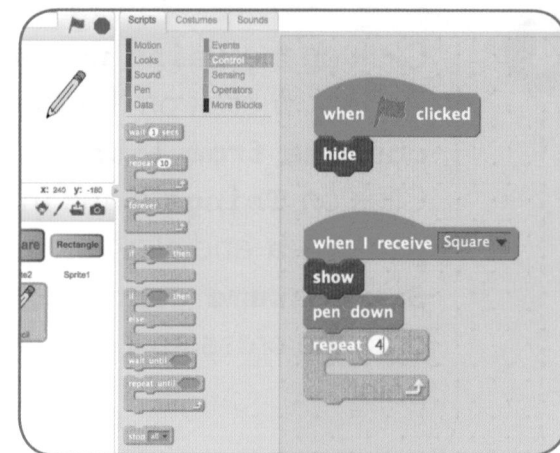

9

Click on **Motion** and drag a **move 10 steps** block into the **repeat...** block of the square script. Type in **100**. Snap on a **turn ↻ 15 degrees** block underneath. Type **90** in the white box. Click on **Control** and snap a **wait 1 secs** block underneath the **repeat** block.

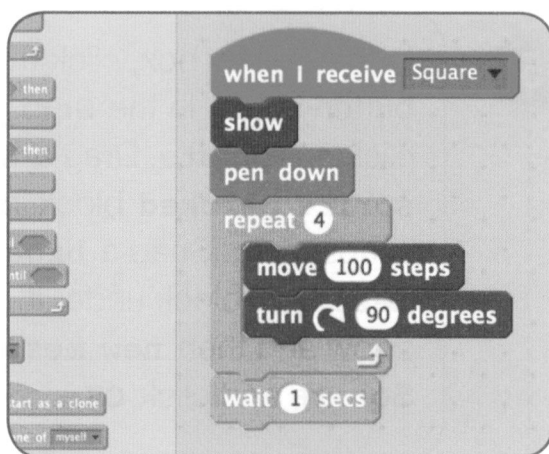

10

Now you need to program what the pencil should do when it receives the *rectangle* message. It will be similar to the algorithm to draw the square except instead of four identical sides, it will need two long and two short sides, as shown in the picture. Use this to help you add the blocks.

11

Click on **Looks** and snap a **hide** block on each script. Then click on **Pen** and add a **clear** block to each script. Check your scripts. What will happen when each sprite is clicked? Click on the green flag icon ⚑ above the preview window. Click on the buttons to see if your code works!

Now try this . . .

- Can you add a **set pen colour to**... block to each script so the square is drawn in red and the rectangle is drawn in blue?

- Can you change each script so the square and rectangle are bigger?

- Can you add a third button, which makes the pencil draw an equilateral triangle?

- Can you add a button that draws a regular hexagon when clicked?

 Design and create a set of cards with different symbols on them to act as buttons. When you hold up a card, see how quickly your partner can follow your request and draw the symbol on the card.

Key words

Can you explain to a partner what these words mean?

script   **program**   **broadcast block**   **message**   **repeat**   **sprite**

How did you do?

Think about what you did in this activity. Did you:

- create a script that creates buttons that draw different shapes when clicked?

- add in **set pen colour to**... blocks to program each button to draw their shape in a different colour?

- change the script to draw shapes that are bigger?

- add in a script for a third button that draws an equilateral triangle?

- add in a script for a fourth button that draws a hexagon?

Activity 2: Scratch Programming a maths quiz

In computer games, the choice a user makes can change what happens. For example, in a quiz, different things can happen when a user chooses a right or wrong answer. You are going to build a maths quiz for younger children.

1 Start by clicking on the cat sprite in the *Sprites* box and then on the **Scripts** tab at the top. Click on **Events** and drag and drop a **when ⚑ clicked** block into the scripts area.

2 Click on the **Looks** category. Snap a **say Hello! for 2 secs** block underneath the **when ⚑ clicked** block. Click in the white box and type **What should the missing numbers be?**.

> Whatever you input into the white box, the sprite will say in a speech bubble as output.

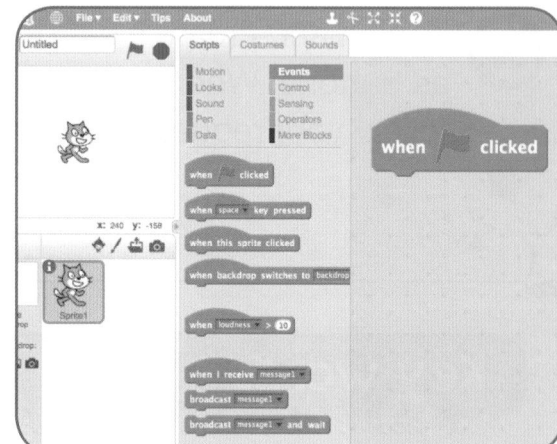

3 Now click on **Sensing**. Snap an **ask What's your name? and wait** block underneath the **say…** block. Click in the white box and type **7 + ? = 10**.

> Using an **ask … and wait** block will allow the user to input an answer to a question by typing it in.

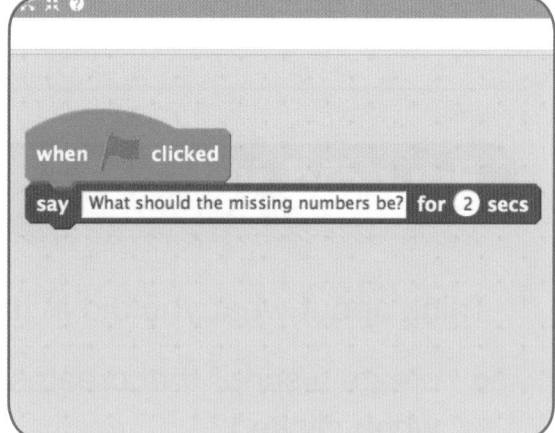

4 Click on **Control** and snap on an **if ... then ... else** block. Click on **Operators** and drag a □ = □ block into the space between *if* and *then*. Click on **Sensing** and drag an **answer** block into the first square of the green operator block. Click in the second box and type **3**.

```
when [flag] clicked
say  What should the missing numbers be?  for 2 secs
ask  7 + ? = 10  and wait
if  < answer = 3 > then
else
```

5 Click on **Looks**. Snap a **say...** block into the first section of the **if ... then ... else** block. Click in the first box and type **You're right!**. Snap another **say...** block into the second section of the **if ... then ... else** block. Type in **That's not right.**.

```
when [flag] clicked
say  What should the missing numbers be?  for 2 secs
ask  7 + ? = 10  and wait
if  < answer = 3 > then
  say  You're right!  for 2 secs
else
  say  That's not right.  for 2 secs
```

6 To make question 2, right-click on the **ask ... and wait** block in the scripts area. Click on **duplicate** in the menu. This will make a copy of all the blocks underneath it. Snap them underneath the **if ... then ... else**.

```
when [flag] clicked
say  What should the missing numbers be?  for 2 secs
ask  7 + ? = 10  and wait
if  < answer = 3 > then
  say  You're right!  for 2 secs
else
  say  That's not right.  for 2 secs
ask  7 + ? = 10  and wait
if  < answer = 3 > then
  say  You're right!  for 2 secs
else
  say  That's not right.  for 2 secs
```

7 Click in the white box on the second **ask ... and wait** block to change the question. Type in **5 + ? = 10**. Click in the white box in the **if answer =** block and change it from *3* to *5*.

```
when [flag] clicked
say  What should the missing numbers be?  for 2 secs
ask  7 + ? = 10  and wait
if  < answer = 3 > then
  say  You're right!  for 2 secs
else
  say  That's not right.  for 2 secs
ask  5 + ? = 10  and wait
if  < answer = 5 > then
  say  You're right!  for 2 secs
else
  say  That's not right.  for 2 secs
```

8 Now for question 3. Right-click on the second **ask … and wait** block in the scripts area. Click on **duplicate** in the menu to make another copy of them. Snap the duplicated blocks underneath the last **if … then … else** block.

9 Click in the white box on the third **ask … and wait** block to change the question. Type in **1 + ? = 10**. Click in the white box in the **if answer =** block underneath it and change it from *5* to **9**. As you have set a new question, you must change the answer to match it.

10 In the **Scripts** tab, click on **Looks**. Snap a final **say…** block underneath. Finally, click in the white box and type **Quiz over!** so the player knows not to expect another question.

11 Look at your code. Can you predict what will happen when you click the green flag icon ⚑ ? Type in correct and incorrect answers to make sure your user will get the right response if they type in a wrong answer.

> You will need to click on the tick to see if your answer was correct.

14

Now try this . . .

- Can you change the three questions to other numbers adding up to 10 and the answer in the **if answer =** block so the quiz still works?

- Can you add another two questions so there are five questions in the quiz?

- Can you add in **change color effect by 25** blocks so when the answer is wrong, the cat turns red? Make sure you program the cat to change back afterwards though, so it doesn't continue to look like all the answers are wrong!

- Can you program the cat so when the answer is correct, the cat turns green? As before, make sure you program it to turn back to its original colour.

 Set up a quiz with a partner. Can you come up with your own conditional actions to show whether the answer is right or wrong? How could you signal this?

Key words

Can you explain to a partner what these words mean?

program   **selection**   **input**   **output**

How did you do?

Think about what you did in this activity. Did you:

- create a script that builds a maths quiz that tells the user if their answer was right?

- change the script to change the questions and answers?

- change the script to add in another two questions?

- program the cat to turn red if the user typed in an incorrect answer?

- program the cat to turn green if a correct answer was given?

Activity 3: Scratch Using variables

Use Scratch at www.scratch.mit.edu. Click *Create* to start!

A variable is something in your code that can change. You are going to build a script for a maths game that uses variables to keep track of the time left and the score. The user must click multiples of 5 to score points.

1 Delete the cat sprite. Click on the **Backdrops** tab. Use the **Fill with color** ◆ tool to make it blue and then click on the scripts area. Now click on the **Paint new backdrop** ∕ icon. Change the new backdrop to graduated black. Click on the **Text** Ⓣ tool. Click on the backdrop and type **Time is up!**.

2 Click on **backdrop1**. Then click on the **Scripts** tab. Click on **Data** and then **Make a Variable**. Type in **score** and click **OK**. Do this again to create a second variable called **time**.

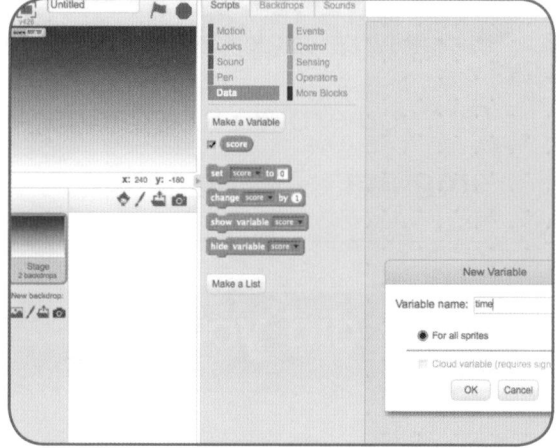

3 Click on the **Choose sprite from library** 👤 icon. Click on **Things** in the menu and then on **Balloon1**. Click **OK**. Now click on the **Costumes** tab. Click on the **Text** tool, then on the balloon sprite and type **5**. Click on the **Scripts** tab.

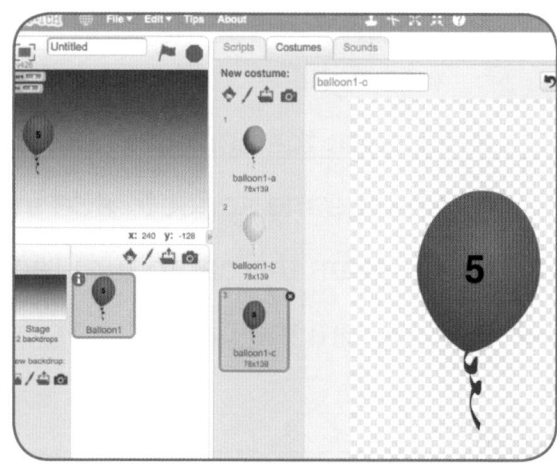

4 Click on **Events** and drag a **when this sprite clicked** block into the scripts area. Click on **Sound**. Snap on a **play sound pop** block. Click on **Data**. Snap on a **change time by 1** block. Change *time* to **score** in the drop-down menu. Type in **10**. Click **Looks** and add a **hide** block.

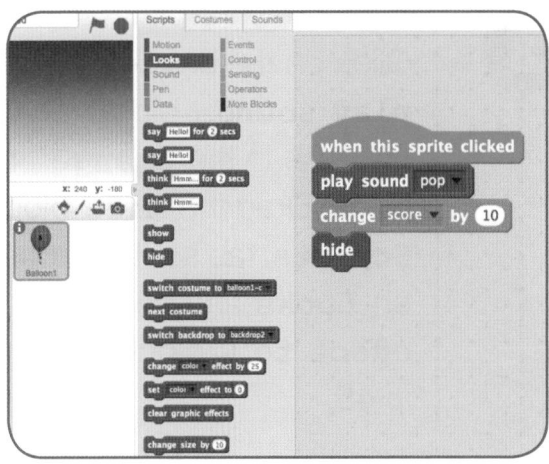

5 Click on **Events** and add a **when ⚑ clicked** block. Then click on **Looks** and snap on a **show** block. Click on **Events** and add a **when backdrop switches to backdrop2** block. From **Looks** snap a **hide** block underneath.

> The user will score 10 points if they click on a multiple of 5.

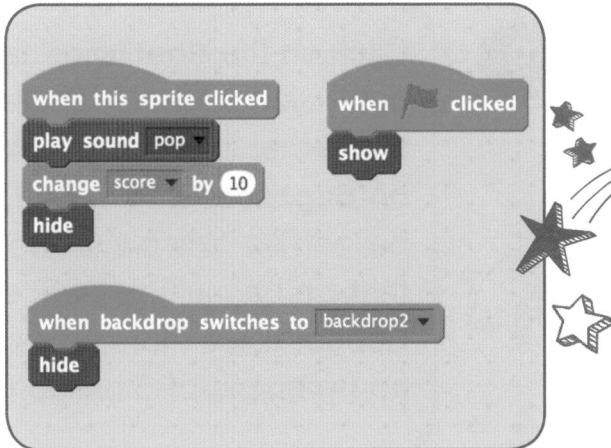

6 Right-click on the balloon sprite in the *Sprites* box. Click on **duplicate**. Change this new balloon so it has another multiple of 5 on it, e.g. 25. Repeat twice more so you have four balloons with multiples of 5 on them.

> Click on the **Costumes** tab and use the **Text** tool to change the number on each new balloon.

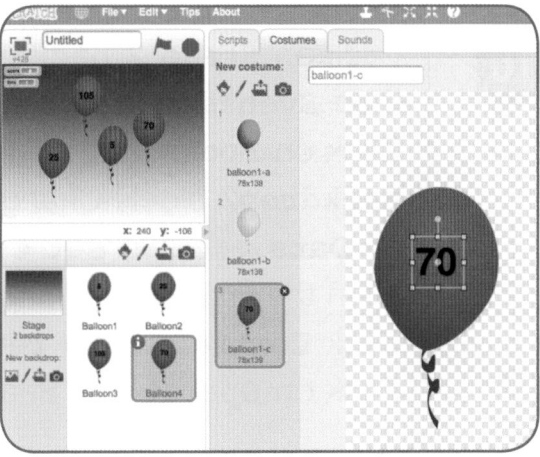

7 Duplicate the balloon again. Change the number to one that isn't a multiple of 5, e.g. 27. Click on the **Sounds** tab, then on the **Choose sound from library** 🔊 icon. Click on **rattle** and **OK**. Click on the **Scripts** tab. This will tell the user they haven't clicked on a multiple of 5.

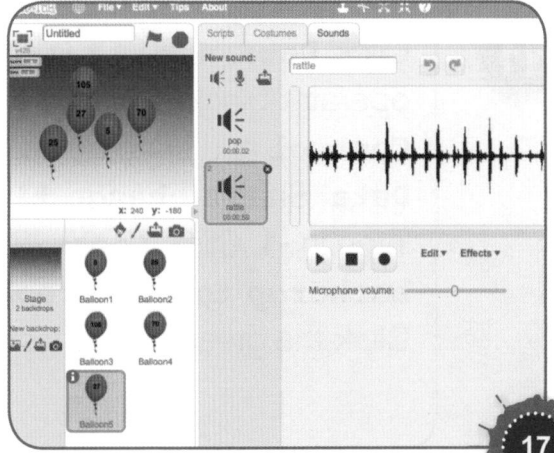

8

Click on the drop-down menu in the **play sound…** block. Change it to **rattle**. In the **change…** block, type in **-5**. Drag the **hide** block over to the **Scripts** tab so it disappears. Click on **Looks** and snap on a **set color effect to 0** block underneath. Type in **45**.

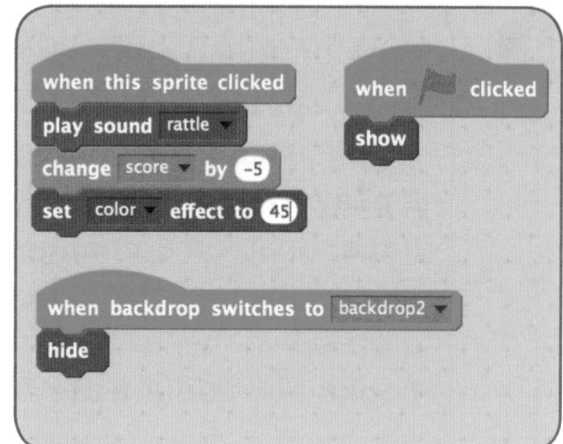

9

Click on the **Costumes** tab and right-click on the *27* sprite (or the sprite that is not a multiple of 5). Click on **duplicate**. Now edit this new balloon so it displays another number that isn't a multiple of 5, e.g. 51. Repeat twice more so you have four non-multiple-of-5 balloons.

10

Click on **Stage 2 backdrops**, then **Scripts**, then **Events**. Add a **when ⚑ clicked** block. Click on **Looks**, add a **switch backdrop to backdrop2** block. Change it to **backdrop1**. Click on **Data**, add two **set time to 0** blocks. Type 10 in the first block. Change the other to **score**. Click **Control**, add a **repeat until…** block. Click on **Operators**. Snap in a ☐ = ☐ block.

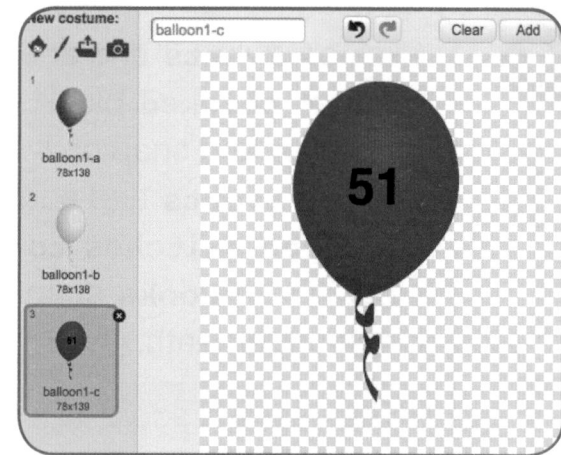

11

Click **Data**. Snap a **time** block into the operator block. Type **0** into the second box. Click **Control** and snap a **wait 1 secs** block. Click **Data**. Snap a **change time…** block underneath. Type in **-1**. Click **Looks**. Snap on a **switch backdrop to backdrop2 and wait** block. Click the green flag to test it.

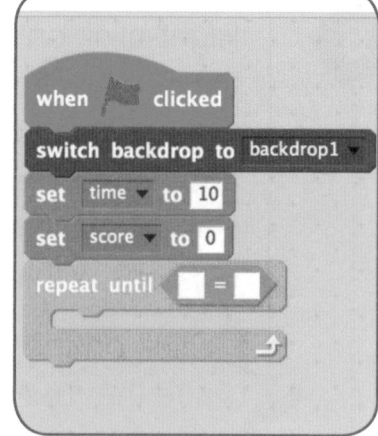

Now try this . . .

- Can you change the scripts so clicking on a multiple-of-5 balloon scores 20 points instead of 10?

- Can you change the script so clicking on a non-multiple-of-5 balloon subtracts 10 points instead of 5?

- Can you add some more balloons to make the game more difficult?

- Can you increase the time limit from 10 seconds to 15 or 20 seconds?

 Play a game with a friend and come up with as many different ways of recording your scores as possible. What other variables might you want to keep track of?

Key words

Can you explain to a partner what these words mean?

program   **script**   **variable**   **output**

How did you do?

Think about what you did in this activity. Did you:

- create a script for a multiple maths game that has a time limit and keeps track of the score?

- change the script to increase the score when a correct balloon is clicked?

- change the script to change the score when an incorrect balloon is clicked?

- add more balloons to the game?

- increase the time limit by adjusting the time condition?

Activity 4: Scratch Using random variables

Use Scratch at www.scratch.mit.edu. Click *Create* to start!

Random variables allow you to create a game that generates questions, such as this maths game which gives the user random pairs of numbers to add up.

1

Add a sprite to go with the cat. Click on the **Choose sprite from library** icon, then on the **Animals** category and select **Dog1**. Click **OK**. Click on the cat sprite, then on the **Scripts** tab and **Events**. Drag a **when space key pressed** block to the scripts area. Repeat for the dog sprite.

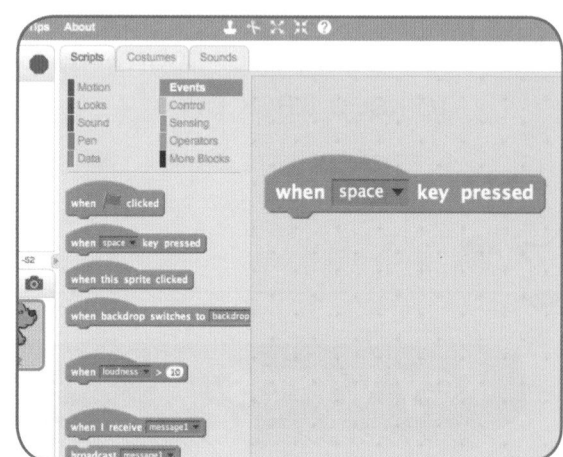

2

Program the cat to generate a random number. Click on the cat sprite. Click on the **Data** category, then **Make a Variable**. Type **Cat's number** in the white box. Click **OK**. Now untick the box next to the new block so the readout disappears from the preview screen.

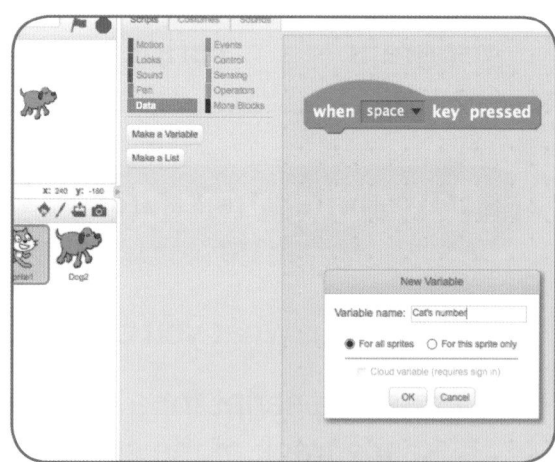

3

We are now going to set what we want the cat's number variable to be, so snap a **set Cat's number to 0** block onto your script.

A variable is a piece of data that can change.

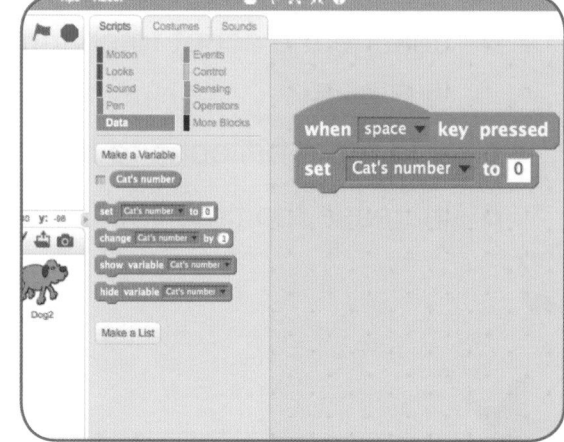

4 We will use a function to return a random number. Click on the **Operators** category. Snap a **pick random 1 to 10** block into the *0* box of the **set Cat's number...** block. As our quiz uses random numbers up to 100, we need to change the last number from *10* to **100**.

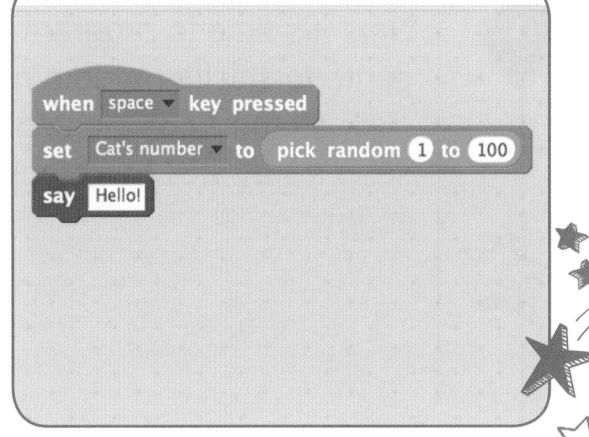

5 Now we can program the cat to say its random number in a speech bubble. Click on the **Looks** category and snap a **say Hello!** block onto your script.

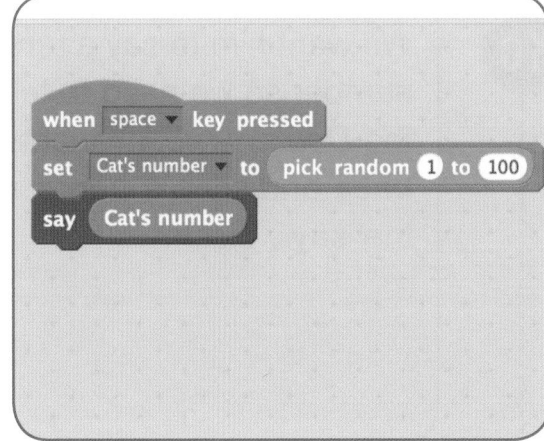

6 Next we need to program the cat to say the *Cat's number* variable: click on **Data** and snap a **Cat's number** block into the **say...** block. Can you predict what will happen when you press the **space bar**? Try pressing it a couple of times. Does the number change each time?

7 It is now time to program the dog to say a random number. He will need his own variable. Click on the dog sprite. Click on **Data**, then **Make a Variable**. Type **Dog's number** in the white box. Click **OK**. Don't forget to untick the box next to the *Dog's number* block.

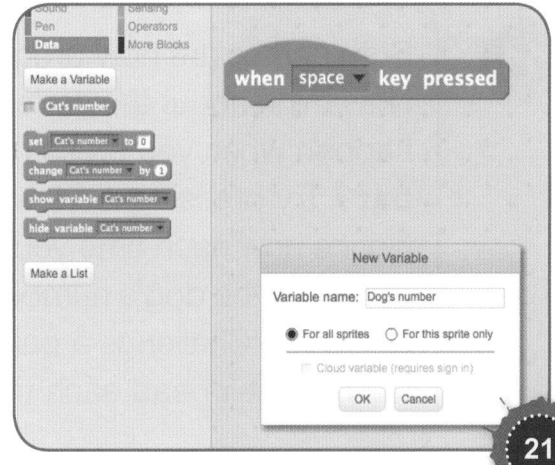

8 Snap a **set Dog's number to 0** onto the dog sprite's script. Click on **Operators** and snap a **pick random 1 to 10** block into the *0* box of the **set ... to ...** block. Remember to change the second number to **100**.

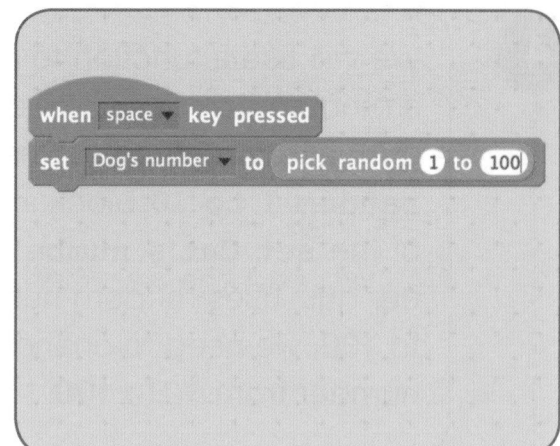

9 Next it's time to program the dog sprite to say its random number, so click on the **Looks** category and snap a **say Hello!** block onto your script.

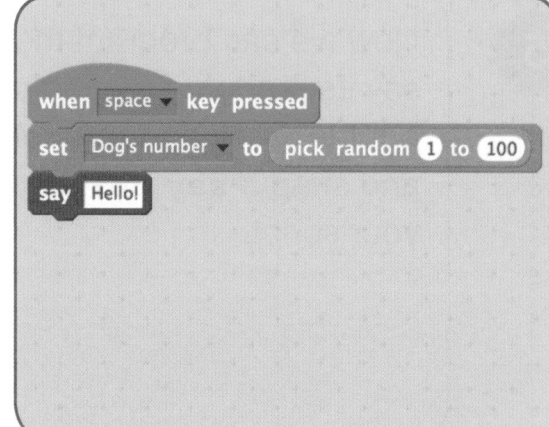

10 We want him to say a random number so we need to tell him to say the *Dog's number* variable. Click on **Data** and snap a **Dog's number** into the **say...** block.

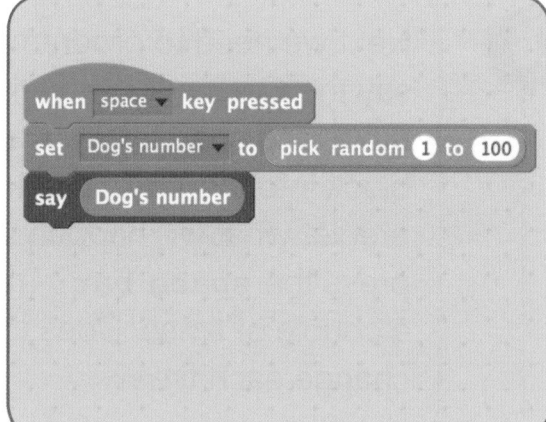

11 Both sprites are now programmed. Now think about the code. What will happen when you press the **space bar**? Try pressing it a few times. Notice how each time you do this, the cat's and the dog's numbers change randomly. Challenge a partner to add them in their head each time.

Now try this . . .

- Can you change the range of numbers generated to include just three-digit numbers?

- Can you add another sprite so the user has three random numbers to add together?

- Can you improve the interface to make it clearer what the game is about and what maths is being tested?

 Can you come up with a different way of generating random numbers for a friend to add together?

Key words

Can you explain to a partner what these words mean?

variable   **program**   **random**   **data**   **generate**

How did you do?

Think about what you did in this activity. Did you:

- create a maths game that generates two random numbers for the user to add?

- change the code so only three-digit numbers are generated?

- add a third sprite so the user has three random numbers to add instead of two?

- improve the interface so the purpose of the game is clearer?

Activity 5: Lightbot
Programming a robot to move

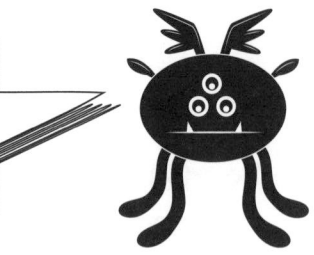

Meet Lightbot, a robot who moves around a world made up of grids. You are going to program Lightbot to walk forward, turn, jump and squat.

1 Click in the address bar of your web browser and type in **http://bit.ly/1iVemu6** to load the Lightbot 2 web page. Click on `Play` and then `Level editor`.

> The Level editor allows you to create and build your own grid for Lightbot.

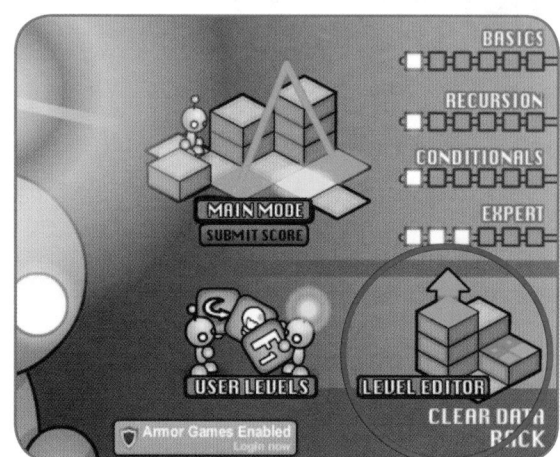

2 Next click on the Lightbot character icon and then on the tile on the left-hand corner of the grid to place him there.

> Your aim is to program Lightbot to light up all the blue squares in the grid.

3 Click on the `change tile color` icon. It looks like a stack of three grey tiles. Then click on the tile on the opposite corner of the grid to Lightbot.

4

Click on the green `raise tile` icon and then on all the tiles three rows in front of Lightbot. This will build a wall.

> Raising these tiles means Lightbot will have to be programmed to jump to reach the blue tile.

5

You are now going to program Lightbot to move to the blue tile and light it up. Click on the green `Test` button to go into play mode.

> Clicking the green `Modify` button takes you back into the Level editor.

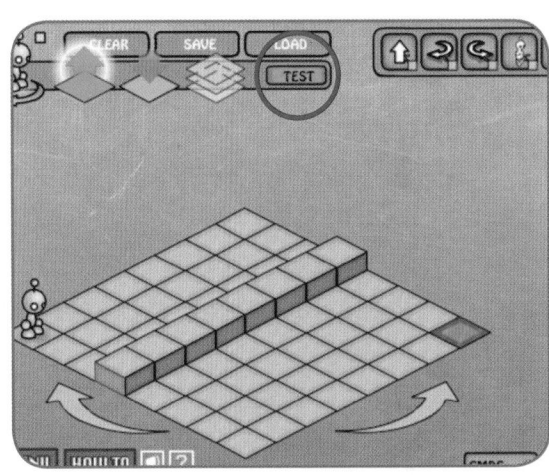

6

You are going to make Lightbot move forward two tiles. Click on the `walk forward` command icon, which looks like an arrow, and then click in the first square in *Main method*. Repeat this in the next square.

7

Click on the `jump` command icon. It looks like a spring. Click in the next empty square in the *Main method* box. Repeat this so there are two `jump` commands.

8

Click on the **walk forward** command icon and then click in the *Main method* box. Do this twice more so there are three **walk forward** commands in a row.

9

Click on the **turn anticlockwise** command icon. The **turn anticlockwise** and **turn clockwise** commands look like turning arrows. Now click in the next empty square in the *Main method* box again.

> Use the **turn** commands to change Lightbot's direction.

10

Add seven **walk forward** commands to the *Main method* box.

> This program will take Lightbot to the blue tile, but to complete the level, he needs to light the blue tile up, not just stand on it.

11

Click on the **light up tile** command icon. It looks like a light bulb. Click in the last square of the *Main method* box. If Lightbot follows this algorithm, will he reach the blue square and light it up? Click on the green **Run** button to try it.

Now try this . . .

- Can you change the program so Lightbot jumps over the wall further along it?

- Can you change the program so Lightbot walks along the wall and then jumps down at the other end?

- Can you use the **`turn clockwise`** command somewhere in the sequence to program Lightbot to reach the blue tile?

- How many possible sequences can you find to complete the level?

-  Program a partner to do a task such as tying their shoelaces or making a paper aeroplane. Can you create some code of your own for the different steps of the task? What symbols could you use?

Key words

Can you explain to a partner what these words mean?

program   **command**   **sequence**   **debug**   **instruct**

How did you do?

Think about what you did in this activity. Did you:

- create a grid for Lightbot to move around on and then sequence a set of commands to program him to light up the blue tile?

- change the program so Lightbot jumps over the wall further along it?

- change the order of the commands so Lightbot walks along the wall before jumping off it?

- change the program to include the **`turn clockwise`** command somewhere along the way?

- find several different solutions to complete the level and program Lightbot to reach the blue tile?

Activity 6: Lightbot
Using functions

In the *Main method* box there are only 16 spaces for code. As grids get more difficult, we need to use more code. Here you will program Lightbot to repeat a sequence using procedures, which can be repeated.

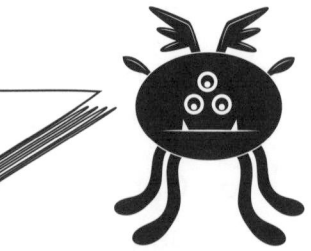

1 Click in the web browser address bar and type **http://bit.ly/1iVemu6**. Click on **Play** and then **Level editor**.

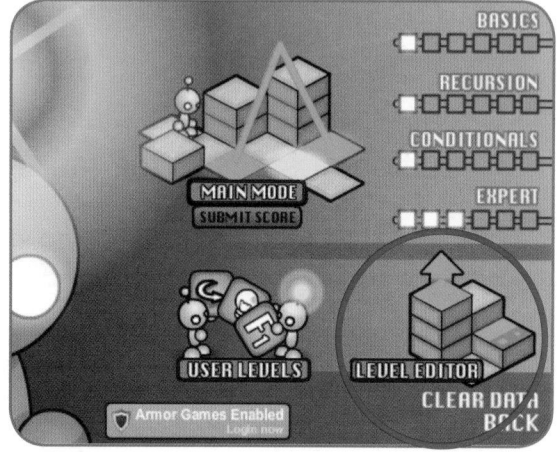

2 Next click on the Lightbot character icon in the tool bar at the top and then click on the tile in the left-hand corner of the grid to place him there. This will be his starting position.

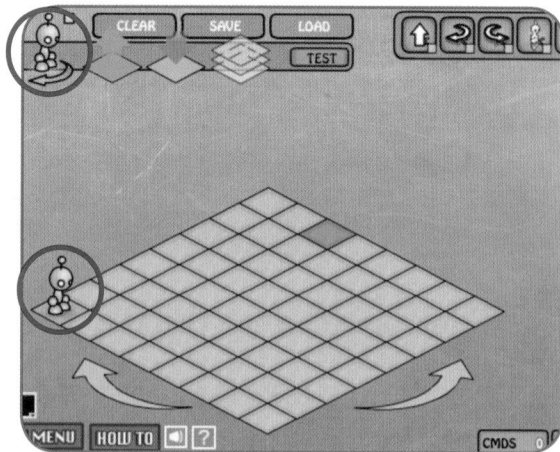

3 Click on the **change tile color** icon. It looks like three grey tiles in a stack. Then click on the three tiles in the other three corners of the grid.

28

4 Use the green `raise tile` icon to build a grid that looks like the one in the picture. It's important all three sides of the grid are the same because your program will use the same command three times.

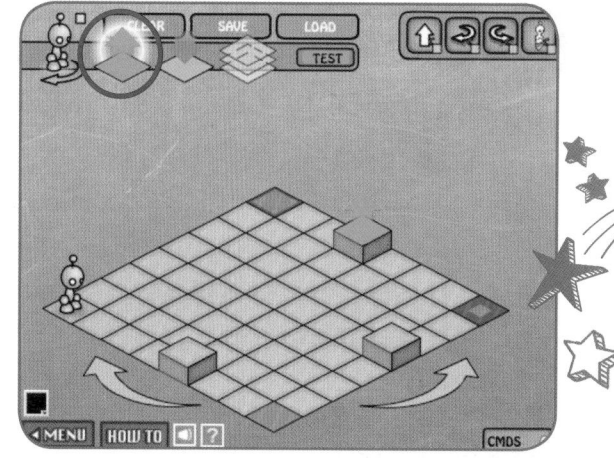

5 We are now going to add commands to the *Function 1* box. These commands will make up a procedure. Click on the green `Test` button. Click on the `walk forward` command icon in the command bar and then in the first square of the *Function 1* box. Do this two more times.

6 Click on the `jump` command icon. Now click in the next empty square in the *Function 1* box. Do this again so there are two `jump` commands. Lightbot needs one `jump` command to jump up onto the raised tile and another to jump down.

7 Add another two `walk forward` commands to the *Function 1* box. Now click on the `light up tile` command icon and click in the last empty square in the *Function 1* box.

8 Click on the **F1** command icon and then into the *Main method* box. Now click on the **turn anticlockwise** command icon and click in the next square. Using the **F1** command tells Lightbot to follow the commands in the *Function 1* box.

9 Now add another **F1** command, a **turn anticlockwise** command and a final **F1** command. There are three **F1** commands in the main program because Lightbot needs to repeat the Function 1 procedure three times.

10 Press the green **Run** button to test the program. There are three **F1** commands in the main program because Lightbot needs to repeat Function 1 three times.

You should now have something that looks like this.

30

Now try this . . .

- Can you remove the three raised tiles and adjust the Function 1 procedure so it still works?

- Can you move the three raised tiles one space forward and then change the Function 1 procedure?

- Can you add in another raised tile next to the one that's already there to each of the three sides and adjust the Function 1 sequence so Lightbot still lights up all the blue tiles?

- Can you create a grid with four blue tiles and four **F1** commands in the main sequence?

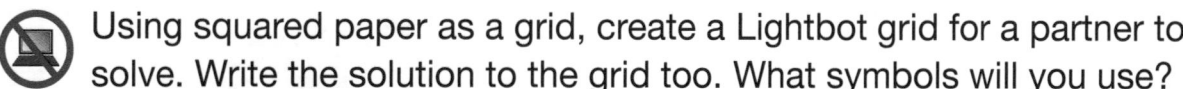 Using squared paper as a grid, create a Lightbot grid for a partner to solve. Write the solution to the grid too. What symbols will you use?

Key words

Can you explain to a partner what these words mean?

command   **program**   **sequence**   **repeat**   **function**

How did you do?

Think about what you did in this activity. Did you:

- create a grid for Lightbot and a program that includes repeating a procedure?

- change the grid to remove the raised tiles and then change the Function 1 procedure so it still works?

- move the raised tiles and change the Function 1 procedure?

- change the Function 1 procedure after adding in another three raised tiles?

- create a grid with four blue tiles to light up and four **F1** commands in the program?

Activity 7: Lightbot
Using more than one function

In the last activity you used a function to repeat instructions. In coding, we call this a procedure. You are going to program Lightbot using two procedures.

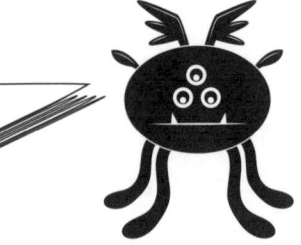

1 Click in the web browser address bar and type **http://bit.ly/1iVemu6**. Click on **Play** and then **Level editor**. Now it's time to build a grid where the two opposite sides are the same.

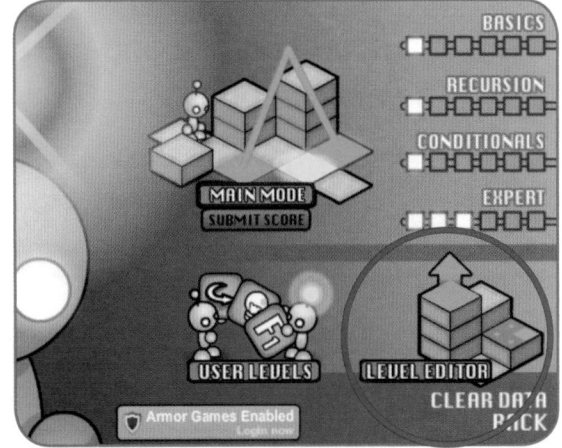

2 Click on the green **raise tile** icon in the tool bar. Click on the third tile along the bottom left of the grid. Then click on the next three tiles to create a wall. Do the same on the other side of the grid.

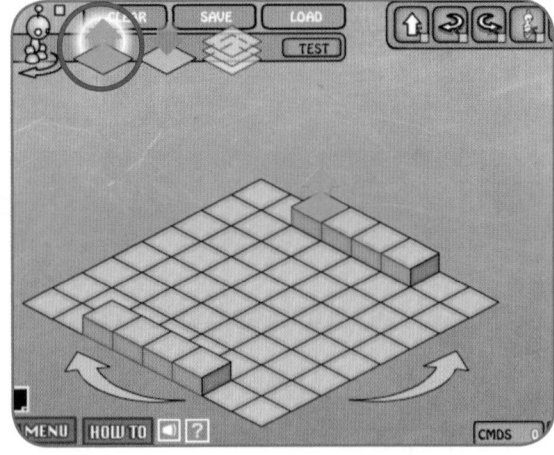

3 Still using the **raise tile** tool, click on the grid to build two L-shaped walls between your walls of four tiles. Make sure the L-shaped walls are facing different ways like they are in the picture.

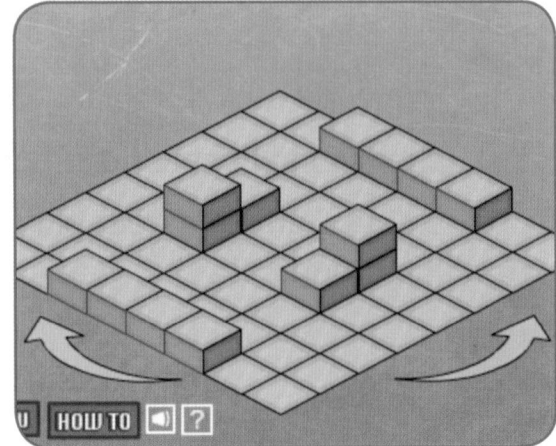

4

Click on the **change tile color** icon (it looks like three grey tiles in a stack). Add blue tiles so they are in the same places as those in the picture. Place Lightbot on the first tile of the first wall. Press the green **Test** button to start programming.

5

Because two sides of the grid are the same, we can repeat two procedures (sets of instructions). For your first procedure, find the *Function 1* box. Add two **walk forward** commands, a **light up tile** command and another **walk forward** command to the box.

6

Add a **turn anticlockwise** command and a **jump** command. This procedure will program Lightbot to move along and light up the blue tiles on the long walls. As it's the same code for both we can repeat Function 1 in the *Main method* program.

7

It's time to build the code for the second procedure, which will program Lightbot to light up the tiles on the smaller walls. Find the *Function 2* box. Add a **walk forward** command, two **jump** commands and a **light up tile** command to the *Function 2* box.

33

8 Finish off the second procedure with another `jump` command, then a `walk forward` command, followed by another `jump` command. End it with a `turn anticlockwise` command. When an `F2` command is placed in the *Main method* program, Lightbot will follow this procedure.

9 Now the two procedures are finished. The first procedure contains the algorithm to move along the long walls. The second procedure contains the algorithm for the shorter walls. Add an `F1` and `F2` command to the *Main method* box. Do this twice.

10 Check your code. Pretend you are Lightbot, following the code in the *Main method* box. Can you predict what will happen? Does the code look right?

11 It's time to test the program. Click the **Run** button. Watch carefully as the commands light up in the *Main method* and *Function* boxes as Lightbot follows them. Does Lightbot light up all the tiles?

Now try this . . .

- Can you move the blue tiles on the L-shaped walls to the first step and adjust Function 2 so it still works?

- Can you add another blue tile on the end of each long wall and change Function 1 so Lightbot still lights up all the tiles?

- Can you use the `lower tile` function to lower one of the tiles on both of the long walls and change Function 1 so it still works?

- Can you create your own grid that requires Lightbot to follow two functions to complete it?

 Try creating an algorithm for a partner to follow that instructs them to create a repeating pattern on squared paper. Can they follow more than one procedure like Lightbot?

Key words

Can you explain to a partner what these words mean?

program   **sequence**   **command**   **function**   **procedure**

How did you do?

Think about what you did in this activity. Did you:

- program Lightbot to light up the tiles by repeating two different functions?

- move the blue tiles to the lower step of the L-shaped walls and change Function 2 so it still works?

- add another blue tile to each long wall and change Function 1 so it still works?

- lower one of the tiles on the long wall and change Function 1 so Lightbot still lights up all the blue tiles?

- create and build your own grid and program Lightbot to complete it by using two functions?

Activity 8: Lightbot
Coding with conditions

Sometimes we want different things to happen when different options are picked. These are called conditions. In this activity you will program Lightbot to perform different commands, but only if he is a certain colour.

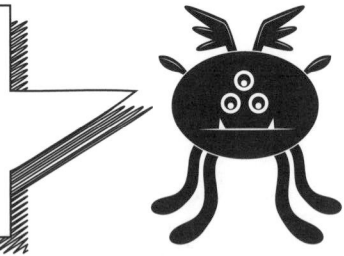

1 Click in the web browser address bar and type **http://bit.ly/1iVemu6**. Click on **Play** and then **Level editor**.

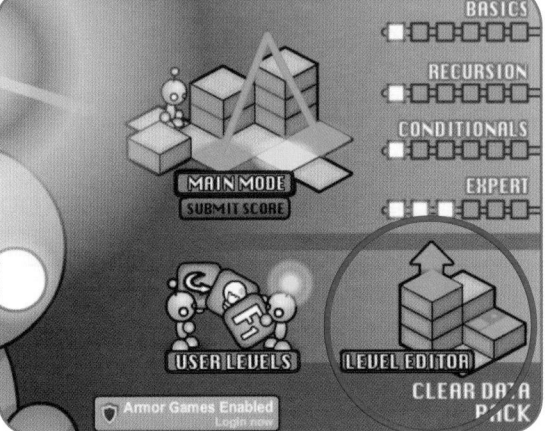

2 Next use the green **raise tile** icon to create a grid like the one in the picture. You are going to create a grid where the **light up tile** tool will only work if Lightbot is purple.

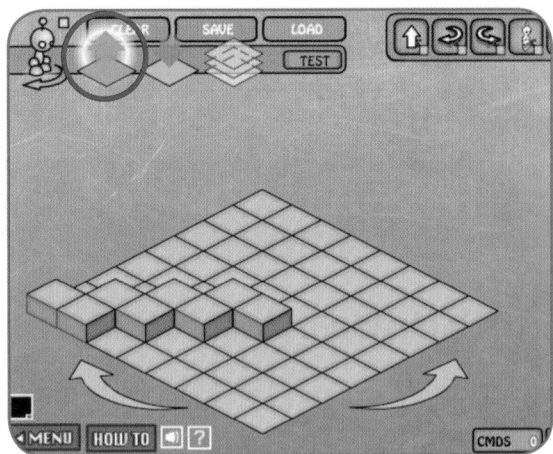

3 Now use the **change tile color** tool to add blue tiles, as shown.

Look at the repeated pattern grid. This means procedures and repetition can be used in the program code too.

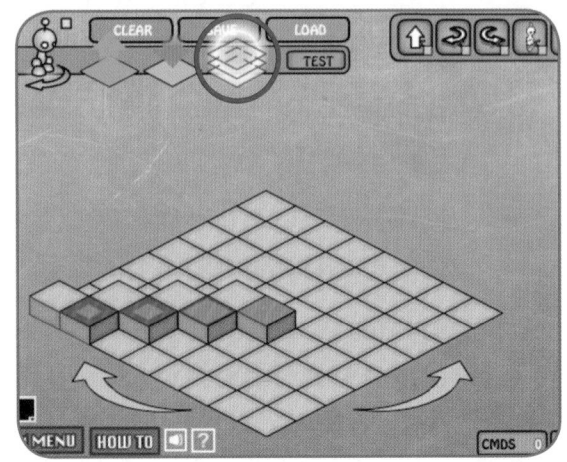

36

4

Use the Lightbot character icon to place Lightbot in the top corner of the grid. This is where Lightbot will start from. Now click on the arrow underneath the Lightbot character icon once to rotate Lightbot 90 degrees clockwise.

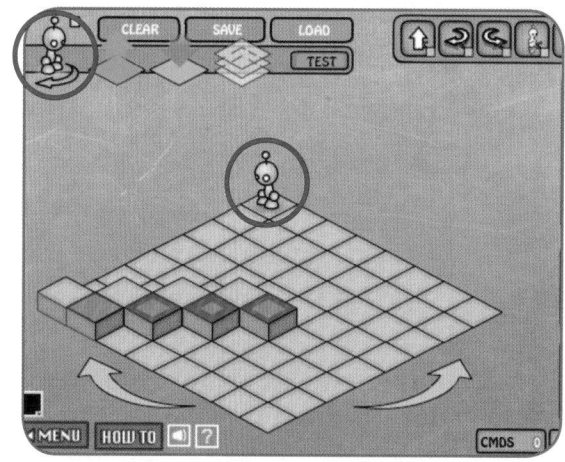

5

Click on the **change tile color** icon. Click five times on the tile in front of Lightbot to turn it orange. Click six times on the next tile to turn it purple. If Lightbot is programmed to light up these tiles, Lightbot will turn that colour.

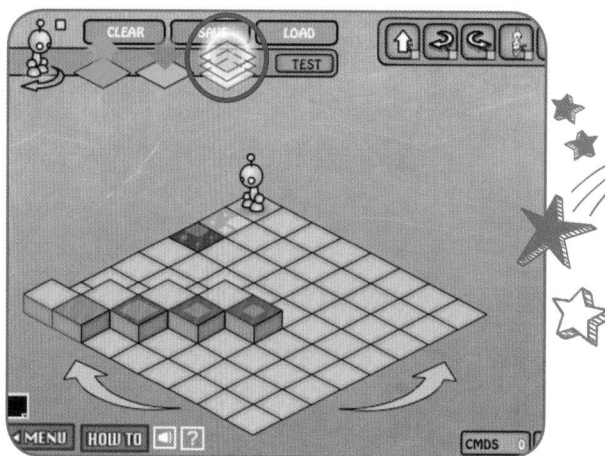

6

You are going to program Function 1 and lock it so it is set for a user to use in play mode. Add these commands to the *Function 1* box:
walk forward, light up tile, turn anticlockwise, walk forward, turn clockwise.

7

Click on the **change color of the command** icon. Now click three times on the **light up tile** command in the *Function 1* box so it turns purple.

The **light up tile** command will only be followed if Lightbot is purple.

37

8

Click the **Test** button to program Lightbot. Add these commands to the *Main method* box: **walk forward**, **light up tile**, five **walk forward**, **jump**, **turn anticlockwise** and four **F1** commands.

> Lightbot will light up the orange tile and he will turn orange.

9

Look at your code. Can you predict what will happen? Click **Run** and watch Lightbot move on the grid. Lightbot doesn't light up the blue tiles because the **light up tile** command is only followed if Lightbot is purple. This sequence programs Lightbot to turn orange.

10

Click on the red **Break** button. You are going to debug the program so Lightbot turns purple and can complete the grid. Click on the **light up tile** command in *Main method*, then on the third square of *Main method*. Add a **walk forward** command to the second square.

11

Look at the new code in the program. Can you predict what will happen? Click on the green **Run** button. Because Lightbot is purple, the **light up tile** command in Function 1 is followed and Lightbot lights up the blue tiles.

Now try this . . .

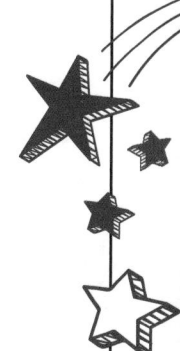

- Can you change the procedure in Function 1 so Lightbot will only follow the `light up tile` command if he is orange?

- Can you change the Function 1 procedure so he will only follow the `turn` commands if he is purple?

- Can you change the condition so Lightbot won't follow any of the Function 1 procedures unless he is purple?

- Can you create a grid and sequence that requires more than one condition?

 Create some 'if' and 'when' *Simon says...* statements with a partner and see if they know when to follow them and when to ignore them, e.g. "If I stand on one leg, then you must sit down."

Key words

Can you explain to a partner what these words mean?

program   **sequence**   **procedure**   **condition**   **function**

How did you do?

Think about what you did in this activity. Did you:

- program Lightbot to follow commands depending on what colour he is?

- change the procedure so Lightbot only lights up the blue tiles if he is orange?

- change the procedure so he only follows the `turn` commands if he is purple?

- change the program so Lightbot only follows Function 1 when he is purple?

- create your own grid that uses more than one condition in the program?

Activity 9: Thimble
Structuring a web page using HTML5 tags

Web pages can be made using a programming language called HTML. In this activity you are going to make a simple web page.

1

Click the address bar of your web browser. Type in **http://thimble.webmaker.org** then press **Enter**.

> In Thimble, the left window is the editor: it shows the HTML code. The right window is a preview of what the web page looks like.

mozilla
Thimble

Editor   Undo   Redo   T T▾ Size

```
1  <!doctype html>
2  <html>
3    <head>
4      <meta charset="utf-8">
5      <title>Your Awesome Webpage created on Thu, Oct 30 2014 2:30
   PM</title>
6    </head>
7    <body>
8      <p>Make something amazing with the web</p>
9    </body>
10 </html>
11
```

2

Delete the text between the *<title>* and *</title>* tags. Type in **Sports Day information**.

> Most HTML tags are made up of an opening < > and closing </> tag. You type your text between them.

Editor   Undo   Redo

```
1  <!doctype html>
2  <html>
3    <head>
4      <meta charset="utf-8">
5      <title>Sports Day information</title>
6    </head>
7    <body>
8      <p>Make something amazing with the web</p>
9    </body>
0  </html>
1
```

3

On line 7, click after the *<body>* tag. Press **Enter**. On line 8, type **<h1>**. Then type **Sports Day information** and the closing tag **</h1>**.

> When you make changes to the code in the editor window, the preview changes to show you what it will look like.

Editor   Undo   Redo

```
1  <!doctype html>
2  <html>
3    <head>
4      <meta charset="utf-8">
5      <title>Sports Day information</title>
6    </head>
7    <body>
8      <h1>Sports Day information</h1>
9      <p>Make something amazing with the web</p>
0    </body>
1  </html>
2
```

4

On line 9, delete the text between the `<p>` and `</p>` tags. Type in **Find out all you need to know** between them instead.

> The `<p>` tags tell the browser to make a new paragraph with the text between them.

```
Editor          Undo       Redo
1  <!doctype html>
2  <html>
3    <head>
4      <meta charset="utf-8">
5      <title>Sports Day information</title>
6    </head>
7    <body>
8      <h1>Sports Day information</h1>
9      <p>Find out all you need to know</p>
10   </body>
11 </html>
12
```

5

On line 9, click after the closing `</p>` and press **Enter**. On line 10, type `<h2>` and then **Dates and Times**. Then type a closing `</h2>` tag. Press **Enter**.

> The `<h2>` tag tells the web browser that this text will be the second-largest heading.

```
Editor          Undo       Redo
1  <!doctype html>
2  <html>
3    <head>
4      <meta charset="utf-8">
5      <title>Sports Day information</title>
6    </head>
7    <body>
8      <h1>Sports Day information</h1>
9      <p>Find out all you need to know</p>
10     <h2>Dates and Times</h2>
11
12   </body>
13 </html>
14
```

6

On line 11, type `<p>`**Date: Monday 1st July**. Press **Enter**. On line 12, type `<br>`**KS1: 9:30-11:00am**. Press **Enter** again. On line 13, type `<br>`**KS2: 1:30-3:00pm**`</p>`.

> The `<br>` tag adds a line break. It has no closing tag and it must be inside a pair of `<p>` and `</p>` tags.

```
Editor          Undo       Redo
1  <!doctype html>
2  <html>
3    <head>
4      <meta charset="utf-8">
5      <title>Sports Day information</title>
6    </head>
7    <body>
8      <h1>Sports Day information</h1>
9      <p>Find out all you need to know</p>
10     <h2>Dates and Times</h2>
11     <p>Date: Monday 1st July
12       <br>KS1: 9:30-11:00am
13       <br>KS2: 1:30-3:00pm</p>
14   </body>
15 </html>
```

7

On line 11, click in front of the word *Date*. Type the opening tag `<strong>`. Click after the colon (:) and type the closing tag `</strong>`.

> Any text between `<strong>` tags will be displayed as bold.

```
Editor          Undo       Redo
1  <!doctype html>
2  <html>
3    <head>
4      <meta charset="utf-8">
5      <title>Sports Day information</title>
6    </head>
7    <body>
8      <h1>Sports Day information</h1>
9      <p>Find out all you need to know</p>
10     <h2>Dates and Times</h2>
11     <p><strong>Date:</strong> Monday 1st July
12       <br>KS1: 9:30-11:00am
13       <br>KS2: 1:30-3:00pm</p>
14   </body>
15 </html>
```

8

On line 12, click between the *
* tag and *KS1*. Type in **<strong>**. Now click after the colon (after *KS1*). Type the closing tag **</strong>**.

```
      Editor                                      ᴛT▾  ⚙
1  <!doctype html>
2  <html>
3    <head>
4      <meta charset="utf-8">
5      <title>Sports Day information</title>
6    </head>
7    <body>
8      <h1> Sports day information</h1>
9      <p>Find out all you need to know</p>
10     <h2>Dates and Times</h2>
11     <p><strong>Date:</strong> Monday 1st July
12       <br><strong>KS1:</strong>| 9:30-11:00am
13       <br>KS2: 1:30-3:00pm</p>
14   </body>
15 </html>
16
```

9

On line 13, click between the *
* tag and *KS2*. Type in **<strong>**. Now click after the colon (after *KS2*). Type the closing tag **</strong>**.

```
      Editor                    ↙ Undo        ↘ Redo
1  <!doctype html>
2  <html>
3    <head>
4      <meta charset="utf-8">
5      <title>Sports Day information</title>
6    </head>
7    <body>
8      <h1>Sports Day information</h1>
9      <p>Find out all you need to know</p>
10     <h2>Dates and Times</h2>
11     <p><strong>Date:</strong> Monday 1st July
12       <br><strong>KS1:</strong> 9:30-11:00am
13       <br><strong>KS2:</strong>| 1:30-3:00pm</p>
14   </body>
15 </html>
```

10

On line 9, click in front of the word *all*. Type **<em>**. Then click after the word *all* and type the closing tag **</em>**.

> Any text between the *<em>* tags will be shown in italics.

```
      Editor                 ↙          ↘      ᴛT▾  ⚙
1  <!doctype html>
2  <html>
3    <head>
4      <meta charset="utf-8">
5      <title>Sports Day information</title>
6    </head>
7    <body>
8      <h1> Sports day information</h1>
9      <p>Find out <em>all</em> you need to
know</p>
10     <h2>Dates and Times</h2>
11     <p><strong>Date:</strong> Monday 1st July
12       <br><strong>KS1:</strong> 9:30-11:00am
13       <br><strong>KS2:</strong> 1:30-3:00pm</p>
14   </body>
```

11

Finally, click before the final bracket in the *<h2>* tag and type so it reads **<h2 style="color:green;">**. Now select all the text on the page. Right-click and click on **Copy**. Then paste it into a document in Word or similar and save it to use next time.

```
      Editor                 ↙          ↘      ᴛT▾   ⚙
1  <!doctype html>
2  <html>
3    <head>
4      <meta charset="utf-8">
5      <title>Sports Day information</title>
6    </head>
7    <body>
8      <h1>Sports Day Information</h1>
9      <p>Find out <em>all</em> you need to know</p>
10     <h2 style="color:green;">Dates and Times</h2>
11     <p><strong>Date:</strong> Monday 1st July
12       <br><strong>KS1:</strong> 9:30-11:00am
13       <br><strong>KS2:</strong> 1:30-3:00pm</p>
14   </body>
15 </html>
16 |
```

Now try this . . .

- Can you make the *Dates and Times* heading smaller by swapping the *<h2>* tags for *<h3>* ones? The *<h3>* tag will display the text as a smaller heading.

- Can you display other words you want to stand out using the *<em>* tag?

- Can you change the colour of the *Dates and Times* subheading from green to another colour?

- Can you change the colour of the main heading?

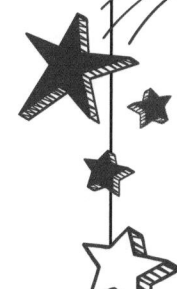

Design a web page of your own. What will it be about? Decide what headings, text and images you would like to include and where they would go on the page.

Key words

Can you explain to a partner what these words mean?

tag   **HTML**   **opening tag**   **closing tag**

How did you do?

Think about what you did in this activity. Did you:

- create a structured web page with different levels of text in it?

- change the code to make the *Dates and Times* heading smaller?

- use the *<em>* tag to display certain text in italics?

- change the code to change the colour of the *Dates and Times* heading?

- change the colour of the main heading?

Activity 10: Thimble
Creating hyperlinks using HTML5

Now you have begun to build your sports day web page, you are going to explore adding hyperlinks to other web pages.

1

Click the address bar of your web browser and type in **http://thimble.webmaker.org** then press **Enter**. You will need to open the document where you saved your code from the last activity. Copy the code and paste it into the Thimble editor.

```
mozilla
Thimble

  Editor          Undo        Redo      T T ▼ Size

1  <!doctype html>
2  <html>
3    <head>
4      <meta charset="utf-8">
5      <title>Sports Day information</title>
6    </head>
7    <body>
8      <h1>Sports Day information</h1>
9      <p>Find out <em>all</em> you need to know</p>
10     <h2 style="color:green;">Dates and Times</h2>
11     <p><strong>Date:</strong> Monday 1st July
12        <br><strong>KS1:</strong> 9:30-11:00am
13        <br><strong>KS2:</strong> 1:30-3:00pm</p>
14    </body>
15  </html>
16
```

2

On line 14, type **<h2>Some great sports links</h2>**. Press **Enter** again.

```
  Editor            ↙        ↘      T T ▼

1  <!doctype html>
2  <html>
3    <head>
4      <meta charset="utf-8">
5      <title>Sports Day information</title>
6    </head>
7    <body>
8      <h1>Sports Day Information</h1>
9      <p>Find out <em>all</em> you need to know</p>
10     <h2 style="color:green;">Dates and Times</h2>
11     <p><strong>Date:</strong> Monday 1st July
12        <br><strong>KS1:</strong> 9:30-11:00am
13        <br><strong>KS2:</strong> 1:30-3:00pm</p>
14     <h2>Some great sports links</h2>
15
16    </body>
17  </html>
```

3

On line 15, type **<ul>**. Press **Enter**. Then on line 16, type **<li>BBC Sports</li>**. Press **Enter**.

The *<ul>* tag creates unordered lists, which look like bullet point lists. Each new item in the list is contained between *<li>* tags.

```
  Editor          Undo        Redo      T T ▼ Si

1  <!doctype html>
2  <html>
3    <head>
4      <meta charset="utf-8">
5      <title>Sports Day information</title>
6    </head>
7    <body>
8      <h1>Sports Day information</h1>
9      <p>Find out <em>all</em> you need to know</p>
10     <h2 style="color:green;">Dates and Times</h2>
11     <p><strong>Date:</strong> Monday 1st July
12        <br><strong>KS1:</strong> 9:30-11:00am
13        <br><strong>KS2:</strong> 1:30-3:00pm</p>
14     <h2>Some great sports links</h2>
15     <ul>
16        <li>BBC Sports</li>
17
18    </body>
19  </html>
```

4

On line 17, type **<li>Sport England</li>**. Then press **Enter**.

The editor displays an exclamation mark symbol when it thinks you have typed incorrect code. It does this here because it is waiting for the closing *</ul>* tag. You'll add that in a minute.

```
Editor          Undo      Redo    TT▾ Si
1  <!doctype html>
2  <html>
3    <head>
4      <meta charset="utf-8">
5      <title>Sports Day information</title>
6    </head>
7    <body>
8      <h1>Sports Day information</h1>
9      <p>Find out <em>all</em> you need to know</p>
10     <h2 style="color:green;">Dates and Times</h2>
11     <p><strong>Date:</strong> Monday 1st July
12       <br><strong>KS1:</strong> 9:30-11:00am
13       <br><strong>KS2:</strong> 1:30-3:00pm</p>
14     <h2>Some great sports links</h2>
15     <ul>
16       <li>BBC Sports</li>
17       <li>Sport England</li>
18
19   </body>
```

5

On line 18, type **<li>Sport Relief </li>**. Press **Enter**. On line 19, type the closing **</ul>** tag. The bulleted list should appear in the preview window.

```
Editor          Undo      Redo    TT▾ Siz
1  <!doctype html>
2  <html>
3    <head>
4      <meta charset="utf-8">
5      <title>Sports Day information</title>
6    </head>
7    <body>
8      <h1>Sports Day information</h1>
9      <p>Find out <em>all</em> you need to know</p>
10     <h2 style="color:green;">Dates and Times</h2>
11     <p><strong>Date:</strong> Monday 1st July
12       <br><strong>KS1:</strong> 9:30-11:00am
13       <br><strong>KS2:</strong> 1:30-3:00pm</p>
14     <h2>Some great sports links</h2>
15     <ul>
16       <li>BBC Sports</li>
17       <li>Sport England</li>
18       <li>Sport Relief</li>
19     </ul>
20   </body>
```

6

Go to line 16. Click between the *<li>* tag and the word *BBC*. Type **<a href="http://www.bbc.co.uk/ sport" target="_blank">**. Click after *Sports* and type the closing **</a>** tag.

Adding *target="_blank"* means the link will open in a new browser window when clicked.

```
Editor          Undo      Redo    TT▾ Size
1  <!doctype html>
2  <html>
3    <head>
4      <meta charset="utf-8">
5      <title>Sports Day information</title>
6    </head>
7    <body>
8      <h1>Sports Day information</h1>
9      <p>Find out <em>all</em> you need to know</p>
10     <h2 style="color:green;">Dates and Times</h2>
11     <p><strong>Date:</strong> Monday 1st July
12       <br><strong>KS1:</strong> 9:30-11:00am
13       <br><strong>KS2:</strong> 1:30-3:00pm</p>
14     <h2>Some great sports links</h2>
15     <ul>
16       <li><a href="http://www.bbc.co.uk/sport" target="_blank">BBC
   Sports</a></li>
17       <li>Sport England</li>
18       <li>Sport Relief</li>
19     </ul>
20   </body>
21 </html>
22
```

7

Go to line 17. Click between the *<li>* tag and the word *Sport*. Then type **<a href="http://www.sportengland. org" target="_blank">**. Click after the word *England* and type the closing **</a>** tag.

```
Editor          Undo      Redo    TT▾ Size
1  <!doctype html>
2  <html>
3    <head>
4      <meta charset="utf-8">
5      <title>Sports Day information</title>
6    </head>
7    <body>
8      <h1>Sports Day information</h1>
9      <p>Find out <em>all</em> you need to know</p>
10     <h2 style="color:green;">Dates and Times</h2>
11     <p><strong>Date:</strong> Monday 1st July
12       <br><strong>KS1:</strong> 9:30-11:00am
13       <br><strong>KS2:</strong> 1:30-3:00pm</p>
14     <h2>Some great sports links</h2>
15     <ul>
16       <li><a href="http://www.bbc.co.uk/sport" target="_blank">BBC
   Sports</a></li>
17       <li><a href="http://www.sportengland.org" target="_blank">Sport
   England</a></li>
18       <li>Sport Relief</li>
19     </ul>
20   </body>
21 </html>
```

8

Go to line 18. Click between the *<li>* tag and the word *Sport*. Then type **<a href="http://www.sportrelief. com" target="_blank">**. Click after the word *Relief* and type the closing **</a>** tag.

```
Editor            ↙ Undo    ↘ Redo    T T▾ Size
1  <!doctype html>
2  <html>
3    <head>
4      <meta charset="utf-8">
5      <title>Sports Day information</title>
6    </head>
7    <body>
8      <h1>Sports Day information</h1>
9      <p>Find out <em>all</em> you need to know</p>
10     <h2 style="color:green;">Dates and Times</h2>
11     <p><strong>Date:</strong> Monday 1st July
12       <br><strong>KS1:</strong> 9:30-11:00am
13       <br><strong>KS2:</strong> 1:30-3:00pm</p>
14     <h2>Some great sports links</h2>
15     <ul>
16       <li><a href="http://www.bbc.co.uk/sport" target="_blank">BBC
   Sports</a></li>
17       <li><a href="http://www.sportengland.org" target="_blank">Sport
   England</a></li>
18       <li><a href="http://sportrelief.com" target="_blank">Sport
   Relief</a></li>
19     </ul>
20   </body>
   </html>
```

9

On line 19, click after the *</ul>* tag and press **Enter**. Type **Why not check out the weather forecast for the day?** on line 20.

```
Editor            ↙ Undo    ↘ Redo    T T▾ Size
1  <!doctype html>
2  <html>
3    <head>
4      <meta charset="utf-8">
5      <title>Sports Day information</title>
6    </head>
7    <body>
8      <h1>Sports Day information</h1>
9      <p>Find out <em>all</em> you need to know</p>
10     <h2 style="color:green;">Dates and Times</h2>
11     <p><strong>Date:</strong> Monday 1st July
12       <br><strong>KS1:</strong> 9:30-11:00am
13       <br><strong>KS2:</strong> 1:30-3:00pm</p>
14     <h2>Some great sports links</h2>
15     <ul>
16       <li><a href="http://www.bbc.co.uk/sport" target="_blank">BBC
   Sports</a></li>
17       <li><a href="http://www.sportengland.org" target="_blank">Sport
   England</a></li>
18       <li><a href="http://sportrelief.com" target="_blank">Sport
   Relief</a></li>
19     </ul>
20     Why not check out the weather forecast for the day?
21   </body>
   </html>
```

10

On line 20, click before the word *weather*. Type **<a href="http:// www.metoffice.gov.uk" target="_ blank">**. Click after *forecast* and type **</a>**.

```
1  <!doctype html>
2  <html>
3    <head>
4      <meta charset="utf-8">
5      <title>Sports Day information</title>
6    </head>
7    <body>
8      <h1>Sports Day information</h1>
9      <p>Find out <em>all</em> you need to know</p>
10     <h2 style="color:green;">Dates and Times</h2>
11     <p><strong>Date:</strong> Monday 1st July
12       <br><strong>KS1:</strong> 9:30-11:00am
13       <br><strong>KS2:</strong> 1:30-3:00pm</p>
14     <h2>Some great sports links</h2>
15     <ul>
16       <li><a href="http://www.bbc.co.uk/sport" target="_blank">BBC
   Sports</a></li>
17       <li><a href="http://www.sportengland.org" target="_blank">Sport
   England</a></li>
18       <li><a href="http://sportrelief.com" target="_blank">Sport
   Relief</a></li>
19     </ul>
20     Why not check out the <a href="http://www.metoffice.gov.uk"
   target="_blank">weather forecast</a> for the day?
21   </body>
22 </html>
```

11

Test your hyperlinks by clicking on them in the preview window. Do they go to the correct pages? Do they open in new browser windows? Finally, select all the text. Right-click and click on **Copy**, then paste it into a document in Word or similar and save it to use next time.

Sports Day information

Find out *all* you need to know

Dates and Times

Date: Monday 1st July
KS1: 9:30-11:00am
KS2: 1:30-3:00pm

Some great sports links

- BBC Sports
- Sport England
- Sport Relief

Why not check out the weather forecast for the day?

Now try this . . .

- Can you change the name and link for the Sport England website to another sports website by changing the code?

- Can you add a fourth link to another sports website to the list?

- Can you add a link to your own school's website at the bottom of the web page?

- Can you add a second unordered list that is a PE kit checklist?

 Sharing links to specific web pages with people can be very useful. If you were to create a web page of your favourite links, what would it include? How would you sort them into groups?

Key words

Can you explain to a partner what these words mean?

HTML   **tag**   **hyperlink**   **unordered list**

How did you do?

Think about what you did in this activity. Did you:

- add hyperlinks to other websites into your web page?

- change the Sport England name and link?

- add code for a fourth link to your list of sports websites?

- add code for a link to your school's own website?

- add another unordered list?

Activity 11: Thimble
Embedding content using HTML5

Your sports day web page now has links and unordered lists, but it needs some images and information about where the school is. In this activity find out how to add a map and an image.

1

Click the address bar of your web browser and type in **http://thimble.webmaker.org** then press **Enter**. Open the document where you saved your code from the last activity. Copy the code and paste it into the Thimble editor. Click at the end of line 9 and press **Enter**.

```
1  <!doctype html>
2  <html>
3    <head>
4      <meta charset="utf-8">
5      <title>Sports Day information</title>
6    </head>
7    <body>
8      <h1>Sports Day information</h1>
9      <p>Find out <em>all</em> you need to know</p>
10     <h2 style="color:green;">Dates and Times</h2>
11     <p><strong>Date:</strong> Monday 1st July
12       <br><strong>KS1:</strong> 9:30-11:00am
13       <br><strong>KS2:</strong> 1:30-3:00pm</p>
14     <h2>Some great sports links</h2>
15     <ul>
16       <li><a href="http://www.bbc.co.uk/sport" target="_blank">BBC
Sports</a></li>
17       <li><a href="http://www.sportengland.org" target="_blank">Sport
England</a></li>
18       <li><a href="http://sportrelief.com" target="_blank">Sport
Relief</a></li>
19     </ul>
20     Why not check out the <a href="http://www.metoffice.gov.uk"
target="_blank">weather forecast</a> for the day?
21   </body>
   </html>
```

2

Open a new browser window and type **http://pixabay.com/en/ stopwatch-time-treadmill-race-259303/** into the address bar. You are going to embed the image on this website into your web page.

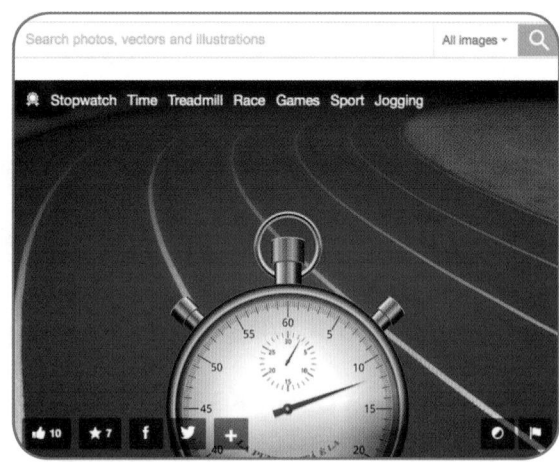

3

Right-click on the image and select **Copy Image Location** or **Copy URL Location** (or similar). Go back to your Thimble window. On line 10 type in **<img src="">**. This tag embeds the image. Click between the "" marks then press **Ctrl** and **v** together. The image should appear in the preview window.

```
     <body>
8      <h1>Sports Day Information</h1>
9      <p>Find out <em>all</em> you need to know</p>
10     <img
src="http://pixabay.com/static/uploads/photo/2014/02/
05/18/12/stopwatch-259303_640.jpg">
11     <h2 style="color:green;">Dates and Times</h2>
12     <p><strong>Date:</strong> Monday 1st July
13       <br><strong>KS1:</strong> 9:30-11:00am
14       <br><strong>KS2:</strong> 1:30-3:00pm</p>
15     <h2>Some great sports links</h2>
16     <ul>
17       <li><a href="http://www.bbc.co.uk/sport"
target="_blank">BBC Sports</a></li>
18       <li><a href="http://www.sportengland.org"
target="_blank">Sport England</a></li>
19       <li><a href="http://sportrelief.com"
target="_blank">Sport Relief</a></li>
20     </ul>
21     Why not check out the <a
href="http://www.metoffice.gov.uk"
target="_blank">weather forecast</a> for the day?
```

4

The image looks quite big so we can add some code into the img tag to resize it. On line 10, click before the closing bracket. Type **height="50%" width="50%"**. This will reduce the image to 50 % of the original size.

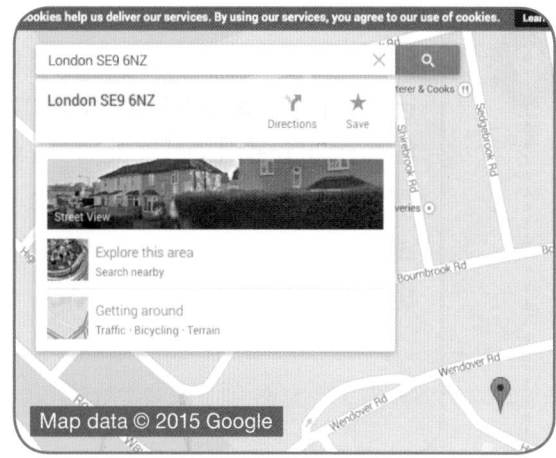

```
1  <!DOCTYPE html>
2  <html>
3    <head>
4      <meta charset="utf-8">
5      <title>Sports Day information</title>
6    </head>
7    <body>
8      <h1>Sports Day information</h1>
9      <p>Find out <em>all</em> you need to know</p>
10     <img
src="http://pixabay.com/static/uploads/photo/2014/02/05/18/12/stopwatch-
259303_640.jpg" height="50%" width="50%">
11     <h2 style="color:green;">Dates and Times</h2>
12     <p><strong>Date:</strong> Monday 1st July
13       <br><strong>KS1:</strong> 9:30-11:00am
14       <br><strong>KS2:</strong> 1:30-3:00pm</p>
15     <h2>Some great sports links</h2>
16     <ul>
17       <li><a href="http://www.bbc.co.uk/sport" target="_blank">BBC
Sports</a></li>
18       <li><a href="http://www.sportengland.org" target="_blank">Sport
England</a></li>
19       <li><a href="http://sportrelief.com" target="_blank">Sport
Relief</a></li>
20     </ul>
21     Why not check out the <a href="http://www.metoffice.gov.uk"
target="_blank">weather forecast</a> for the day?
22   </body>
23 </html>
```

5

Open a new browser window. In the address bar, type **http://maps.google.co.uk**. Type your school's postcode in the search box. Check with your teacher that this follows the e-safety policy: you must be very careful about sharing your location online.

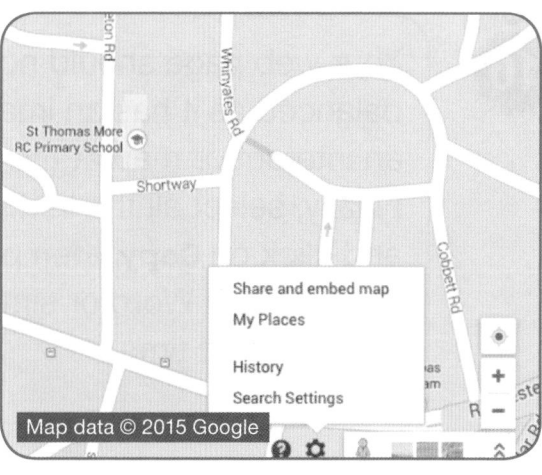

6

Click on the **Settings** icon at the bottom right of the window and then click on **Share and embed map**. The **Settings** icon looks like a cog.

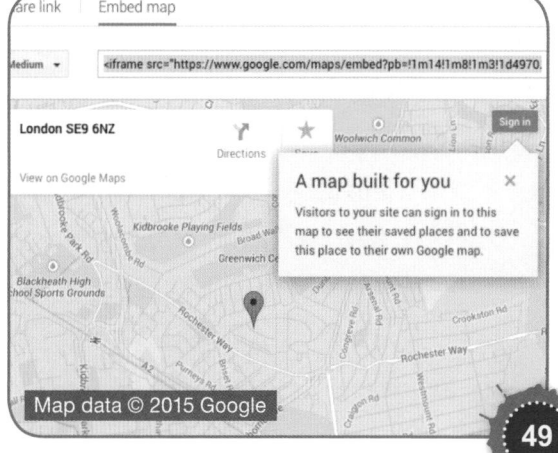

7

Click on the **Embed map** tab in the new window that appears. Click in the long box so the code is highlighted. Press **Ctrl** and **C** together to copy the embed code.

> The *iframe* tag allows you to embed a document within another HTML document.

8

Click back on the tab with Thimble open in your browser. On line 21, click after the question mark and press **Enter**. Type in **
<h2>Find us </h2>**.

```
6    <title>Sports Day information</title>
     </head>
     <body>
8      <h1>Sports Day information</h1>
9      <p>Find out <em>all</em> you need to know</p>
10     <img
src="http://pixabay.com/static/uploads/photo/2014/02/05/18/12/stopwatch
259303_640.jpg" height="50%" width="50%">
11     <h2 style="color:green;">Dates and Times</h2>
12     <p><strong>Date:</strong> Monday 1st July
13       <br><strong>KS1:</strong> 9:30-11:00am
14       <br><strong>KS2:</strong> 1:30-3:00pm</p>
15     <h2>Some great sports links</h2>
16     <ul>
17       <li><a href="http://www.bbc.co.uk/sport" target="_blank">BBC
Sports</a></li>
18       <li><a href="http://www.sportengland.org" target="_blank">Sport
England</a></li>
19       <li><a href="http://sportrelief.com" target="_blank">Sport
Relief</a></li>
20     </ul>
21     Why not check out the <a href="http://www.metoffice.gov.uk"
target="_blank">weather forecast</a> for the day?
22     <br><h2>Find us</h2>
23     </body>
24 </html>
```

9

Press **Enter** so you are on line 23. Press **Ctrl** and **V** together to paste the map embed code. A Google map of your school's address should now appear in the preview window, under the *Find us* subheading.

```
259303_640.jpg height="50%" width="50%">
11     <h2 style="color:green;">Dates and Times</h2>
12     <p><strong>Date:</strong> Monday 1st July
13       <br><strong>KS1:</strong> 9:30-11:00am
14       <br><strong>KS2:</strong> 1:30-3:00pm</p>
15     <h2>Some great sports links</h2>
16     <ul>
17       <li><a href="http://www.bbc.co.uk/sport" target="_blank">BBC
Sports</a></li>
18       <li><a href="http://www.sportengland.org" target="_blank">Sport
England</a></li>
19       <li><a href="http://sportrelief.com" target="_blank">Sport
Relief</a></li>
20     </ul>
21     Why not check out the <a href="http://www.metoffice.gov.uk"
target="_blank">weather forecast</a> for the day?
22     <br><h2>Find us</h2>
23     <iframe src="https://www.google.com/maps/embed?
pb=!1m14!1m8!1m3!1d4970.628135625042!2d0.031545671350690925!3d51.4707491
519936!3m2!1i1024!2i768!4f13.1!3m3!1m2!1s0x47d8a9a89f24f489%3A0x89d68f25
7ff09e!2sLondon+SE9+6NZ!5e0!3m2!1sen!2suk!4v1414684422108" width="600"
height="450" frameborder="0" style="border:0"></iframe>
24     </body>
25 </html>
26
```

10

Your web page should now look more balanced as it has an image, text and an interactive map at the bottom. Finally, select all the text. Right-click and click on **Copy**, then paste it into a document in Word or similar and save it to use next time.

Some great sports links

- BBC Sports
- Sport England
- Sport Relief

Why not check out the weather forecast for the day?

Find us

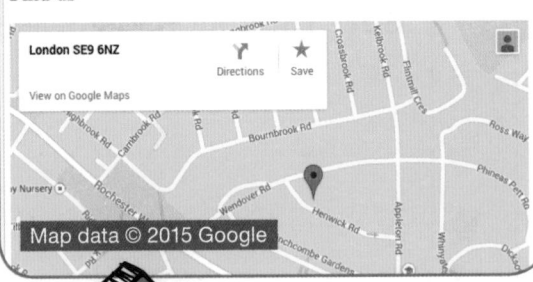

You should now have something that looks like this.

Now try this . . .

- Can you add other images?

- Can you change the size of the image to 75%?

- Can you alter the Google Maps embed code to change the width and the height of the Google map?

- Can you use cut and paste to change the position of the Google map on your page?

 Think about the map and the image you have embedded into your web page. How are they different?

Key words

Can you explain to a partner what these words mean?

code   HTML   embed   tag   <iframe>   <img>

How did you do?

Think about what you did in this activity. Did you:

- add an image and a Google map to your web page?

- add other images?

- change the size of the image?

- change the code to change the size of the Google map?

- change the position of the Google map by cutting and pasting the code?

Activity 12: Thimble
Creating tables using HTML5

You need to add some important information to your sports day web page: the order of events. A table is the best way to present information like this.

1 Click the address bar of your web browser and type in **http://thimble.webmaker.org** then press **Enter**. You will need to open the document where you saved your code from the last activity. Copy the code and then paste it into the Thimble editor.

2 On line 14, click after the code and press **Enter**. On line 15, type **<table>**. Then press **Enter** again.

> The *<table>* tag tells the browser where a table begins. At the end it will need a closing *</table>* tag.

3 On line 16, type **<tr>**. This is the tag for a table row. Press **Enter**. On line 17, type **<th>Event</th>**. Press **Enter**. *Event* is going to be the first column heading in the table.

4

On line 18, type **<th>Time</th>**. Then press **Enter**. *Time* will be the second column heading.

```
13      <br><strong>KS1:</strong> 9:30-11:00am
14      <br><strong>KS2:</strong> 1:30-3:00pm</p>
15    <table>
16     <tr>
17        <th>Event</th>
18        <th>Time</th>
19
20    <h2>Some great sports links</h2>
21    <ul>
22        <li><a href="http://www.bbc.co.uk/sport" targ
  </li>
23        <li><a href="http://www.sportengland.org" t
  </li>
24        <li><a href="http://sportrelief.com" targe
25    </ul>
26    Why not check out the <a href="http://www.metof
  target="_blank">weather forecast</a> for the day?
27    <br><h2>Find us</h2>
28    <iframe src="https://www.google.com/maps/embed?
  pb=!1m14!1m8!1m3!1d4970.628135625042!2d0.0315456717
```

5

On line 19, type **<th>Year group </th>**, then type the closing tag **</tr>**. Press **Enter** again.

```
10    <img
  src="http://pixabay.com/static/uploads/photo/2014/02/05/18/12/stop
  ch-259303_640.jpg" height="50%" width="50%">
11    <h2 style="color:green;">Dates and Times</h2>
12    <p><strong>Date:</strong> Monday 1st July
13      <br><strong>KS1:</strong> 9:30-11:00am
14      <br><strong>KS2:</strong> 1:30-3:00pm</p>
15    <table>
16     <tr>
17        <th>Event</th>
18        <th>Time</th>
19        <th>Year group</th></tr>
20
21    <h2>Some great sports links</h2>
22    <ul>
23        <li><a href="http://www.bbc.co.uk/sport" target="_blank">BBC
  Sports</a></li>
24        <li><a href="http://www.sportengland.org" target="_blank">Sp
  England</a></li>
25        <li><a href="http://sportrelief.com" target="_blank">Sport
  Relief</a></li>
26    </ul>
27    Why not check out the <a href="http://www.metoffice.gov.uk"
  target="_blank">weather forecast</a> for the day?
28    <br><h2>Find us</h2>
29    <iframe src="https://www.google.com/maps/embed?
```

6

On line 20, type **<tr>**. Press **Enter**. Type **<td>Egg and spoon race </td>** on line 21. Press **Enter** again. Type **<td>9:45am</td>** and press **Enter**. On line 23, type **<td>Year 1 </td>**. Press **Enter**.

> *<td>* is the tag used for a standard cell in a table. *<tr>* is only used for the headings in a table.

```
10    <img
  src="http://pixabay.com/static/uploads/photo/2014/02/05/18/12/s
  ch-259303_640.jpg" height="50%" width="50%">
11    <h2 style="color:green;">Dates and Times</h2>
12    <p><strong>Date:</strong> Monday 1st July
13      <br><strong>KS1:</strong> 9:30-11:00am
14      <br><strong>KS2:</strong> 1:30-3:00pm</p>
15    <table>
16     <tr>
17        <th>Event</th>
18        <th>Time</th>
19        <th>Year group</th></tr>
20     <tr>
21        <td>Egg and spoon race</td>
22        <td>9:45am</td>
23        <td>Year 1</td>
24
25    <h2>Some great sports links</h2>
26    <ul>
27        <li><a href="http://www.bbc.co.uk/sport" target="_blank">
  Sports</a></li>
28        <li><a href="http://www.sportengland.org" target="_blank"
  England</a></li>
29        <li><a href="http://sportrelief.com" target="_blank">Spo
  Relief</a></li>
```

7

On line 24, type **</tr>**. Press **Enter** and type an opening **<tr>** tag on line 25. Press **Enter** again. On line 26, type **<td>Relay</td>**. Press **Enter**. On line 27, type **<td>10:00am </td>**. Press **Enter** again. Type **<td>Year 2</td>** on line 28. Press **Enter**.

```
10    src="http://pixabay.com/static/uploads/photo/2014/02/05/18/12/stopw
  ch-259303_640.jpg" height="50%" width="50%">
11    <h2 style="color:green;">Dates and Times</h2>
12    <p><strong>Date:</strong> Monday 1st July
13      <br><strong>KS1:</strong> 9:30-11:00am
14      <br><strong>KS2:</strong> 1:30-3:00pm</p>
15    <table>
16     <tr>
17        <th>Event</th>
18        <th>Time</th>
19        <th>Year group</th></tr>
20     <tr>
21        <td>Egg and spoon race</td>
22        <td>9:45am</td>
23        <td>Year 1</td>
24     </tr>
25     <tr>
26        <td>Relay</td>
27        <td>10:00am</td>
28        <td>Year 2</td>
29
30    <h2>Some great sports links</h2>
31    <ul>
32        <li><a href="http://www.bbc.co.uk/sport" target="_blank">BBC
  Sports</a></li>
33        <li><a href="http://www.sportengland.org" target="_blank"
  England</a></li>
```

8

On line 29, type **</tr>**. Press **Enter**. On line 30, type **<tr>** and press **Enter**. On line 31, type **<td>Fancy dress race</td>**. Press **Enter**. On line 32, type **<td>10:15am</td>**. Press **Enter**, then type **<td>Year 2</td>** on line 33. Press **Enter** once more.

```
17          <th>Event</th>
18          <th>Time</th>
19          <th>Year Group</th></tr>
20        <tr>
21          <td>Egg and spoon race</td>
22          <td>9:45am</td>
23          <td>Year 1</td>
24        </tr>
25        <tr>
26          <td>Relay</td>
27          <td>10:00am</td>
28          <td>Year 2</td>
29        </tr>
30        <tr>
31          <td>Fancy dress race</td>
32          <td>10:15am</td>
33          <td>Year 2</td>
34          |
35      <h2>Some great sports links</h2>
```

9

On line 34, type **</tr>**. Press **Enter** and then type **</table>** on line 35.

> The *</table>* tag tells the browser where the table ends.

```
15      <table>
16        <tr>
17          <th>Event</th>
18          <th>Time</th>
19          <th>Year group</th></tr>
20        <tr>
21          <td>Egg and spoon race</td>
22          <td>9:45am</td>
23          <td>Year 1</td>
24        </tr>
25        <tr>
26          <td>Relay</td>
27          <td>10:00am</td>
28          <td>Year 2</td>
29        </tr>
30        <tr>
31          <td>Fancy dress race</td>
32          <td>10:15am</td>
33          <td>Year 2</td>
34        </tr>
35      </table>|
36      <h2>Some great sports links</h2>
37      <ul>
38        <li><a href="http://www.bbc.co.uk/sport"
```

10

On line 3, click after *<head>* and press **Enter**. On line 4, type **<style>**. Press **Enter**. On line 5, type **table,th,td**. Press **Enter**. Type **{border: 1px solid black;}** on line 6. Press **Enter**. Type **</style>** on line 7.

> This code formats the table grid lines.

```
    Editor                    ↙    ↘    ᴛTᐁ            ⚙

1  <!doctype html>
2  <html>
3    <head>
4      <style>
5        table,th,td
6        {border: 1px solid black;}
7      </style>
8      <meta charset="utf-8">
9      <title>Sports Day information</title>
10   </head>
11   <body>
12     <h1>Sports Day information</h1>
13     <p>Find out <em>all</em> you need to know</p>
14     <img
    src="http://pixabay.com/static/uploads/photo/2014/02/05/18/12/st
    opwatch-259303_640.jpg" height="50%" width="50%">
15     <h2 style="color:green;">Dates and Times</h2>
16     <p><strong>Date:</strong> Monday 1st July
17       <br><strong>KS1:</strong> 9:30-11:00am
18       <br><strong>KS2:</strong> 1:30-3:00pm</p>
19     <table>
20       <tr>
```

11

Finally, view your complete sports day page, which now has an order of events table in it too. Copy and paste the code into a Word document and save it in case you want to add to it later in Thimble.

Dates and Times

Date: Monday 1st July
KS1: 9:30-11:00am
KS2: 1:30-3:00pm

Event	Time	Year Group
Egg and spoon race	9:45am	Year 1
Relay	10:00am	Year 2
Fancy dress race	10:15am	Year 2

Now try this . . .

- Can you change the text that says *Egg and spoon race* to *100m sprint*?

- Can you change the table formatting so the grid lines are blue instead of black?

- Try adding another row to the table with the following information about another race: *Three-legged race, 10:30am* and *Year 2*.

- Can you add another column to the table with the heading *Location*?

 Design a web page for a different purpose. Think about how you could apply all the elements you have learned, such as formatting text, coding hyperlinks, embedding images and creating tables.

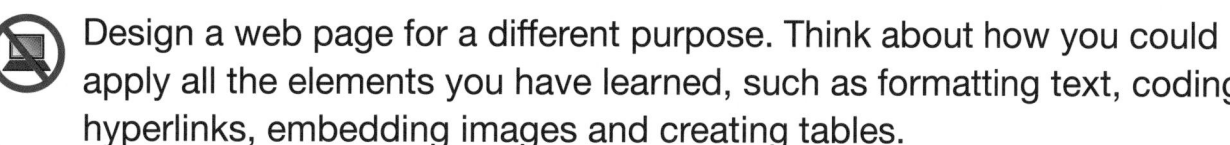

Key words

Can you explain to a partner what these words mean?

HTML   **code**   **tag**   **formatting**   **style**

How did you do?

Think about what you did in this activity. Did you:

- add a table to your web page?

- change the code so the grid lines are blue instead of black?

- change the code to change some of the text in the table?

- add code for another row to the table?

- add code for another column to the table?

Glossary

- **Broadcast block:** allows you to send a message in Scratch to activate other commands or scripts.

- **Closing tag:** this tells the web browser where a tag ends. The closing tag must include a forward slash.

- **Code:** the commands or program you write using a programming language.

- **Command:** an instruction given to an object or character to make something happen.

- **Condition:** something that is true or false. E.g.: Number 6 is in the box. True or false?

- **Data:** information that can be stored, collected or changed.

- **Debug:** to find and get rid of errors within code.

- **Embed:** insert something (for example, an image) from somewhere else (for example, a different web page).

- **Formatting:** to change the style of text, e.g. alignment, spacing and bold.

- **Function:** a small section of code that makes a specific process happen, and importantly returns a result (or answer).

- **Generate:** to produce something.

- **HTML:** Hypertext Markup Language – the language used to create web pages.

- **Hyperlink:** a link that takes a user to another document or web page, or to another part of a document.

- **<iframe>:** the HTML tag for a frame in a web page that can contain an image or another web page.

- **<img>:** the HTML tag for an image within a web page.

- **Input:** information given to a computer to make something happen (e.g. a mouse click or button press).

- **Instruct:** to tell someone or something to do a specific task.

- **Message:** a (short) communication sent from one source to another.

- **Opening tag:** this tells the web browser where a tag starts.

- **Output:** something that a computer produces when given an instruction, e.g. an on-screen image, a sound or vibration.

- **Procedure:** a small section of code that makes a specific process happen.

- **Program:**
  1. a sequence of instructions to perform a task or solve a problem, using programming language (noun)
  2. to create or change a program (verb).

- **Random:** not in order.

- **Repeat:** take a certain command (or set of commands) and follow the instruction again (and again).

- **Script:** a set of commands that are followed by a program.

- **Selection:**
  1. the act of selecting something
  2. one thing or a group of things that have been selected.

- **Sequence:** a set of commands that run one after another.

- **Sprite:** an object or character that can be programmed.

- **Style:** the way that text is presented – e.g. colour, underlined, bold.

- **Tag:** code used to label the content in an HTML document.

- **Unordered list:** this <ul> tag allows you to create bulleted lists in HTML.

- **Variable:** a piece of data that can be changed to produce a different result.